The Rise of the Hellenistic Kingdoms 336–250 BC

For Jeremy Day

The Rise of the
Hellenistic Kingdoms
336–250 BC

Philip Matyszak

Pen & Sword
MILITARY

First published in Great Britain in 2019 by
Pen & Sword Military
An imprint of
Pen & Sword Books Ltd
Yorkshire – Philadelphia

Copyright © Philip Matyszak 2019

ISBN 978 1 47387 476 3

The right of Philip Matyszak to be identified as Author of this work
has been asserted by him in accordance with the Copyright, Designs
and Patents Act 1988.

A CIP catalogue record for this book is
available from the British Library.

Printed and bound in the UK by TJ International Ltd,
Padstow, Cornwall.

Pen & Sword Books Limited incorporates the imprints of Atlas,
Archaeology, Aviation, Discovery, Family History, Fiction, History,
Maritime, Military, Military Classics, Politics, Select, Transport,
True Crime, Air World, Frontline Publishing, Leo Cooper, Remember
When, Seaforth Publishing, The Praetorian Press, Wharncliffe
Local History, Wharncliffe Transport, Wharncliffe True Crime
and White Owl.

For a complete list of Pen & Sword titles please contact

PEN & SWORD BOOKS LIMITED
47 Church Street, Barnsley, South Yorkshire, S70 2AS, England
E-mail: enquiries@pen-and-sword.co.uk
Website: www.pen-and-sword.co.uk

Or

PEN AND SWORD BOOKS
1950 Lawrence Rd, Havertown, PA 19083, USA
E-mail: Uspen-and-sword@casematepublishers.com
Website: www.penandswordbooks.com

Contents

List of Plates

Macedon and Greece.

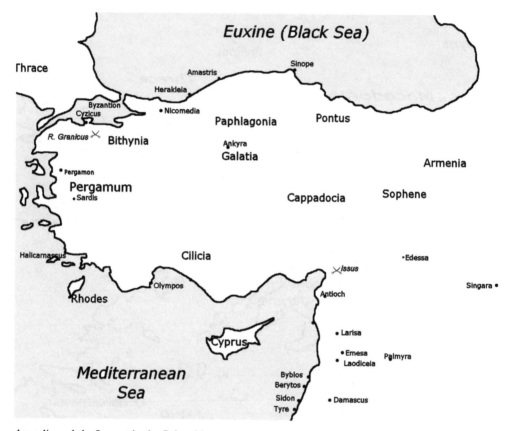

Anatolia and the Levant in the Seleucid era.

The Eastern Seleucid Empire by ethnicity.

The Egypt of Ptolemy II.

Introduction

This is not only an introduction to this book, but for many people it will be also an introduction to the Hellenistic era as a whole. In the modern world, whether in books, films or university courses, the Hellenistic era is a Cinderella, unfairly regarded as a space-filler between the glories of Classical Greece (800–300 BC) and the rise of the Roman Empire.

As one scholar has observed, the problem with the Hellenistic era is that later historians keep projecting on to it the issues of their own time. In the West, nineteenth-century historians did the era a disservice by dissecting the racial differences between the 'degenerate' native peoples and their Greek overlords, and acted as cheerleaders for the 'civilizing' of the 'Eastern barbarians'. (Not that there is much actual evidence for a Greek mission to Hellenize the East, or that the Hellenistic kings were particularly racist. They were certainly chauvinist, and convinced of the superiority of their own culture, but they seem to have accepted anyone else who shared that culture, regardless of ethnic origin.)

In the later twentieth century Hellenism was also tarred with the brush of colonialism. (After all, Greek settlements outside Greece are what gave a 'colony' its name.) In the Hellenistic era we had a people from a European country ruling over native peoples – possibly even 'oppressed native peoples' – and encouraging floods of settlers from their 'home country' who made an indelible mark on the culture of the peoples whom they were exploiting. That's the classic definition of colonialism, and colonialism as practised in the nineteenth and twentieth centuries is correctly regarded as a wrong inflicted by Europe upon the rest of the world. So here again, perceptions of the Hellenistic world have been affected by reinterpretation drawn from the experiences of later eras.

All this has been enough to mark an enthusiast for the Hellenistic era as a neo-colonialist with suspiciously racist overtones. To this we add the fact that many scholars in the Hellenistic era itself believed that the great days of Greek intellectual advancement were gone and their main endeavour should be to study and preserve the glories of the past. The philosophy of the Hellenistic era was marked by an air of general disillusionment with government. The great democratic experiments of the Classical era had basically failed. The world had reverted to the tried-and-true systems of monarchical rule that had been working since before the Bronze Age. Theories of government such as Plato's 'Republic' were out, replaced by a kind of weary cynicism and a turning inward to the contemplation of the self.

So why study the Hellenistic era? Perhaps the best reason, which learned papers and academic disdain have successfully managed to obscure, is the important fact that the Hellenistic era is great fun. For those who like their history in primary colours with larger-than-life characters, exotic locations and desperate skulduggery (preferably involving princesses and pirates), the Hellenistic era richly rewards the explorer. It is after all a period that encompasses almost three centuries and geographically it extends from Buddhist temples in Samarkand, past the ziggurats of Babylon to sanctuaries and pyramids along the Nile. Never before or since did the classical world cover an area so diverse, exotic and colourful.

Certainly there are important issues to explore in the interaction of cultures, and the effect of imposed urbanism on rural native populations. But there are also barbarian Celtic invaders charging across the landscape to clash with kings equipped with war elephants imported from India. There are epic battles and sieges, collapsing kingdoms and spice-laden camel caravans arriving from the orient. Oppression there certainly was. Regular visits from the four horsemen of famine, plague, war and death were a part of everyday life (especially war, of which the Hellenistic kings were regrettably fond).

However, anyone familiar with the history of the Middle East will note that despite this, relatively speaking the Hellenistic era was quieter than most. Many people got on with happy, productive lives under a government that was for the times, enlightened and efficient. Far from an impression of miserable drudgery, there is a refreshing dynamism and optimism about the period.

'Decline' is sometimes a matter of perception. Hellenistic Greek scholars, obsessed with the low quality of lyric poetry in their day, managed to overlook the fact that the intellectual excitement of their age was invested in the crude mechanical businesses of engineering, architecture, physics and mathematics.

Among the other Hellenic breakthroughs we find spectacles, automobiles (Heron of Alexandria's self-propelled cart), the piston pump, the steam engine and the first slot machine. Not to mention mathematicians who calculated the diameter of the Earth to within a five per cent margin of error, and whose discoveries on irrational and prime numbers remain well beyond the grasp of the average modern historian.

We have the first star charts, the development of taxonomy to classify animal species, and the first library indexes. There were huge advances in medicine and understanding human anatomy, while geography moved from the 'here be dragons' phase to detailed maps – all this while Alexandrian intellectuals were bemoaning the fact that their generation had not produced a single tragic playwright to match those of the classical era.

It is not the fault of the Hellenistic Greeks that most of the intellectual breakthroughs of their era were not followed up. Theirs was a brief flowering in a foreign field that was probably doomed even had it not been crushed by the unimaginative Roman monolith. Yet that part of the Hellenistic kingdoms which remained forever out of the reach of Rome gives us a glimpse of what might have been.

One of the great things about Hellenistic culture was that it was essentially humanistic and inclusive. That culture was at its most tenuous in the far east of the Hellenistic world, at the foothills of the Himalayas and on the banks of the River Indus. Yet here, where the Roman legions never set foot and Hellenistic culture was severed from its western roots, it was not violently overthrown. Instead Greek and native cultures seem to have gently melded, taking the best of each until what remained was something unique and the common property of all. And as it happened, the intellectual treasures of the ancient world were less preserved in monasteries than in the great eastern libraries of Islam. What might have happened if the western kingdoms underwent the same gradual transformation?

The Hellenistic kingdoms of Macedon and Egypt did not collapse through internal inadequacies. They fell because the Romans pushed them – hard. We can now only speculate what cultures might have slowly developed and the course that human civilization might have taken if the Hellenistic era had not been so brutally curtailed.

In this volume we tell the first part of the story of the Hellenistic kingdoms. Starting with the rise of Macedon to hegemony over Greece, we trace the conquests of Alexander and the creation of the Greek east. Once Alexander has died in Babylon, the story settles into a prolonged period of wars, diplomatic double-cross, dynastic intrigue and murder. Once the dust has settled, Alexander's empire has become three major kingdoms plus independent odds and ends. In the second part of the book we survey those kingdoms, their strengths, their weaknesses and their contribution to later civilization. The rough end date is 250 BC, just before the death of Ptolemy II. By then the Hellenistic kingdoms were well established, and to those living there it must have seemed that they would last forever.

Chapter 1

Before Alexander

The Hellenistic kingdoms did not spring into being from nowhere. Outside Greece itself, Hellenism was seldom more than a bright superstructure built upon the edifice of civilizations that had already flourished for hundreds, if not thousands of years. When we read that a huge swathe of land from Afghanistan to Egypt became 'Greek' within a generation, it is necessary also to accept that most of that land did not become Greek at all.

After the conquests of Alexander, the rulers of the ancient empires changed language and culture, but not a lot was different for the peasants in the field. They continued farming in the age-old manner, worshipped their ancient gods and paid their customary taxes to the local headman or priest who forwarded them to the relevant authorities, whoever they may have been.

One reason for the success of the Hellenistic kingdoms – and this book will argue that the Hellenistic kingdoms were massively successful – was that the Greek rulers of Egypt, Anatolia, Persia, and points east did not try to change the peoples they ruled. Unlike some of the more shameful practices of later settler cultures, the Greeks had no programme of 'de-nativization' and made little effort to convert the peoples they ruled to their own way of life.

On the whole, the Hellenistic rulers took the vastly different economies and cultures of their new realms and left them pretty much as they found them. This is not to say that the Greeks themselves 'went native' – instead a sort of symbiosis developed between Greek and native cultures. In some places, such as Judea, this coexistence was uncomfortable and violent. In other places, such as Bactria, local and Greek cultures eventually fused into a unique blend that took much of the best from each.

Consequently we cannot understand the Hellenistic kingdoms without understanding those parts that were not Hellenistic at all, for the non-

Hellenic parts were the fundamental underpinning of each kingdom. Consequently, the Seleucid and Ptolemaic kingdoms faced vastly different challenges because the Seleucid and Ptolemaic kings ruled peoples with vastly different societies and economies. These people had very different ideas of what a ruler was and different expectations of what that ruler should be doing. The other Hellenistic kingdom, Macedon, was different again. Nevertheless, like the Seleucids and Ptolemies, the Macedonian kings had the same problem – how to govern a people who were socially and politically alien.

The same issues manifested themselves in different ways in each kingdom. For example, Macedon had the difficult job of managing the rebellious and unruly city-states of southern Greece. The Seleucids faced the entrenched and obdurate resistance of the Jews, and the Ptolemies grappled with independent-minded secessionists beyond the first cataract of the Nile.

On the other hand, the Greeks had always been unruly, the Jews objected to being ruled by anybody – Greek or otherwise – and the Persians had faced regular rebellions from the Egyptians long before the Ptolemies inherited the problem. The eruption of Alexander into the ancient kingdoms of the Middle East merely put a new complexion on the situation. It did not change the fundamentals, but it did add a new layer of complexity.

Therefore, before we come to Alexander and the growth of the Hellenistic kingdoms it is necessary to begin with an examination of the lands which Alexander took over and which his successors ruled – starting with the land that Alexander himself came from.

Macedon

Thanks to Alexander and his father Philip II, we tend to think of the Macedonians as expansionist conquerors. After all, it was Macedon which subdued Greece by military force and Macedonian phalangites led the Greeks in their conquest of Asia. Yet it is very probable that the Macedonians saw themselves very differently. For most of its existence Macedonia was a relatively small kingdom beset by numerous and powerful foes. If the Macedonians were some of the toughest fighters in the ancient world, it was because nature and geography had left them with little choice but to fight or die.

Macedonia evolved from settlements which grew along the river systems which link the mountains of north-eastern Greece with the Aegean Sea. These mountain ranges provided some shelter from invading armies, but nevertheless the Macedonians were far less protected from barbarian hordes than the Greeks to the south. Athens, Thebes and the other city states of fifth-century Greece were free to develop their glittering intellectual achievements in part because they were sheltered from barbarian invasion by the massif of the Olympus range – and by Macedonia itself.

This latter fact caused the Macedonians a degree of bitterness. In the course of defending themselves the Macedonians necessarily had to defend the Greeks to the south. That is, to get at Athens and the other states of central Greece, an invader had first to conquer the Macedonians. If the Macedonians defended themselves from conquest they automatically defended the rest of Greece. For their efforts in protecting Greek civilization from destruction, the Macedonians were sneered at by their more cultured cousins to the south as uncultured semi-barbarians. During the fifth century the Macedonians were not even considered 'Greek' enough to participate in the Olympic Games (though an exception was made for the royal family because tradition claimed that the Macedonian ruling dynasty came from Argos).

Yet it was the Macedonians who had to fight off massive incursions from Thracian tribes who regularly pillaged the countryside around Mount Pangaion. Often these pillaging raids coincided with Paeonian raids on the other side of the kingdom, for Macedon's barbarian neighbours had long ago figured out that the Macedonian army could not be everywhere at once.

On occasion the Paeonians were themselves as much victims as the Macedonians, because they had as neighbours the Epirots, the Illyrians and the Dardanians. All of these peoples were wild and warlike and more than happy to charge through and pillage Paeonia before descending on the more settled Macedonians. These incursions were a regular feature of Macedonian history – massive plundering raids that could only be thrown back with all the resources that the state could muster..

The stress that barbarian assaults placed on the kingdom was instrumental in bringing Alexander the Great to power. The Illyrians came close to conquering Macedonia in 393 BC, just under half a century before Alexander's birth. The king at the time was Alexander's grandfather, Amyntas III. He was driven from his kingdom and only regained it with help from his southern neighbours in (usually) friendly Thessaly. After the death of Amyntas, his oldest son, Alexander II, continued the struggle with these Illyrian invaders. Once Alexander died young, his brother Perdiccas III took over and was promptly killed in battle with the barbarians. This cleared the path to power for the youngest of Amyntas' three sons. This was Philip II, the father of Alexander the Great.

Alexander II, the uncle of his more famous namesake, was not killed in battle with the Illyrians. He was assassinated by a rival who intended to rule as a regent for Perdiccas. However, Perdiccas had the would-be regent assassinated in his turn before he took power and went off to be killed by the Illyrians. This combination of regular barbarian incursions and lethal palace politics made the life of Macedonian kings both interesting and short. Since Philip II was also eventually assassinated, we can understand why his son Alexander the Great had a less than trusting disposition when he ascended the Macedonian throne in his turn.

As well as barbarians seeking plunder, and ambitious rivals scheming to take the throne, Macedon's rulers also had to contend with the more systematic assaults of more organized civilizations. One such was the massive and expansionist Persian Empire. The westward expansion of the Persian Empire at the start of the fifth century BC at one point forced the Macedonians to become a subject kingdom. It was largely because Macedonia on this occasion failed in its usual role as a bulwark against foreign invasion that the Greeks to the south were forced to fight the Persians at Thermopylae and Salamis. Once the Persians had been thrown back, the Macedonians found that they also had to contend with the aggressive expansion of their southern neighbours into Thrace and the Chalcidice Peninsula.

The regular strain of fighting against extinction by near-overwhelming odds explains why Macedon remained a kingdom instead of evolving into the independent city-states of southern Greece. Even the peoples of southern Greece had briefly united under Spartan leadership to defeat the Persian invasion. However, for the southern Greeks the need to unite against an invader was an almost unprecedented event. The Macedonian people had to continually fight off invasions and consequently could not ever afford the luxury of being divided amongst themselves. Their kings were essentially war-leaders and they needed the entire nation behind them if the kingdom was to survive.

The rigours of fifth-century life meant that the Macedonians had to be centralized, organized and highly aggressive. Therefore when an opportunity for expansion presented itself in the fourth century, the Macedonian kingdom was more than equal to the challenge.

This opportunity came because the southern Greeks, while they had little need to fight off foreign attackers, were very good at fighting among themselves. As previously described, the only major foreign invasion of the fifth century BC was the attempted Persian conquest. This the Greeks had united to repel. With the Persians beaten back, the Athenians took over the leadership of the Greek alliance against Persia and used it not to fight the Persians but for the aggrandizement of Athens. This aggrandizement included expansion in northern Greece, into areas which the indignant Macedonians regarded as being in their usual sphere of influence.

The Spartans and their allies eventually crushed the nascent Athenian empire in a series of conflicts usually lumped together under the name of the Peloponnesian War, which started in 460 BC (or 431 depending on which conflicts are included). Having beaten the Athenians into submission, the Spartans in turn strove for the hegemony of Greece and were in turn defeated by the Thebans.

These internecine wars between the city-states of Greece resulted in almost a century of sustained, high-intensity conflict which drained the country of military manpower and economic resources. Meanwhile the Macedonians had been doing rather well for themselves.

The initial impetus was provided by Amyntas III. In between beating and getting beaten up by the Illyrians, this highly competent ruler managed to expand the kingdom and establish a number of profitable trade routes with his southern neighbours. As a part of his interactions with the southern states, Amyntas sent his youngest son Philip as a hostage to Thebes, at that time a rising power in central Greece. Somewhere between a prisoner and an honoured guest, Philip had a front-row seat of the techniques the enterprising and energetic Thebans used to revitalize their army and crush the Spartans.

As the exigencies of ruling Macedon killed off his brothers in short order, Philip returned to Macedon – initially as regent for the son of his deceased brother Perdiccas. (That son, 'King' Amyntas IV, never ruled for a day in his rather brief life. Philip simply ignored the boy's claim to the throne and began ruling as Philip II. When Alexander the Great succeeded his father he had Amyntas executed as a matter of course. Macedonian kings had little tolerance for rivals.)

Philip was a highly capable diplomat and soldier, and had inherited a kingdom with a solid economy. The Illyrians were temporarily subdued after the energetic efforts of Philip's predecessors and the Thracians, though still a threat, were partly distracted by Athenian expansion into their territory. With a mixture of subtle diplomacy and brute force Philip subdued the Thracians and then turned on the Athenians. With the east of his kingdom secure, Philip went west and inflicted a major defeat on the Illyrians. This convincing show of military prowess made diplomacy with the Epirots and Dardanians a lot easier, while the friendship of the dangerous Molossian tribe was secured by Philip's marriage to the princess Olympias.

Free to turn east once more, Philip took up where the Athenians had left off, and began securing the natural resources of Thrace for his kingdom. By 356 BC Macedon and Philip were doing well. In that year Philip took Krenides in Thrace and also possession of the town's highly lucrative gold mines. In July, Philip received on the same day the satisfactory news that his horses had won the chariot races at the Olympic Games and that his wife Olympias had given him a son and heir. Philip renamed Krenides Philippi after himself, and he called his new-born son Alexander after his dead brother Alexander II.

With the barbarians to east and west either cowed by military force or constrained by diplomatic ties, Philip was free to turn his attention southward. As always, the Macedonian intent was primarily defensive, and Philip was thinking of the long term. Macedon had once been a subject kingdom of the Persians and that fact was both deeply resented by the Macedonians and a topic of constant reproach from the rest of

Greece. Philip intended to turn the tables. Even if he did not intend to make the Persians a subject kingdom, he certainly planned to drive the frontiers of the Persian Empire far back enough to prevent Persia from ever threatening Macedonia again.

It may have seemed impossibly ambitious of tiny Macedon to take on the Persian Empire. At a rough estimate, Macedonia was some 50,000 square kilometres in area, while the Persian Empire sprawled over 5,500,000 square kilometres. In other words, Philip proposed to take on an enemy state over a hundred times larger than his own. This was not so much David versus Goliath as David versus Goliath, Goliath's brothers, cousins, uncles and the rest.

Philip reckoned he had a reasonable chance of success in any case. This was due to two factors. Firstly, the Greeks had spent the previous century demonstrating time and again that their soldiers could out-fight the Persians. This was not because the Persians lacked organization or courage, but because their army was optimized to fight the very different enemies they faced elsewhere. Though essential against steppe horsemen, the bowmen who were the mainstay of the Persian army were outmatched against heavily armoured Greek hoplites.

Furthermore, Philip had further optimized his army by equipping his soldiers with the *sarissa*, a long pike that allowed the direct participation of even those in the third rank of the tightly-packed infantry phalanx. This gave Philip's foot units weight and depth that his enemies could not match, and this in turn allowed greater freedom of manoeuvre for Macedonia's superb cavalry.

The second point was that Philip did not intend Macedon to fight the Persians alone. He intended to take the rest of Greece into battle with him. In other words, Philip intended to put Macedon at the head of a Hellenic League of the type that Sparta had headed against the Persians 150 years previously.

Philip was well aware that, like the Spartans, he would not be able to lead the Greeks against the Persians if his state could not demonstrate that it also led the Greeks in military prowess. Philip was more than happy to forcibly demonstrate that prowess to the rest of Greece. The Athenians, and to a lesser degree the Thebans and Spartans had been a constant thorn in his side. These states resented the growing power to the north and constantly tried to wrest from Philip his control of parts of Thrace, Thessaly and the Chalcidice Peninsula.

Philip began the methodical subjugation of the Greek cities of both mainland Greece and the northern Aegean. His was an opportunistic campaign of conquest which picked off targets when the circumstances were right. He also inserted himself into a typically messy ongoing spat between southern Greek cities which is today dignified by the name of the 'Sacred Wars'. One result of his involvement in these wars was that after the Macedonians practically massacred the Phocian people in battle they took the Phocians' place in an ancient religious association called the Amphictyonic League.

This was important, because membership of the Amphictyonic League was only open to Greeks. By admitting the Macedonians to the League the rest of Greece conceded – reluctantly and at the point of a sword, but nevertheless conceded – that the Macedonians were now officially Greeks.

Not only did this make Philip a legitimate leader of any future Greek alliance, but in the long term it established an important principle. A person could self-identify as 'Greek', and so long as anyone so professing demonstrated the linguistic ability and cultural awareness equivalent to that of any other Hellene, the rest of the Greek world accepted that Greekness, even if neither that particular 'Greek' nor his ancestors had been anywhere near the Greek mainland. After Philip, being Greek was no longer a matter of genetic but of cultural heritage.

Neither the Thebans nor the Athenians accepted Macedonian dominance quietly, and it was inevitable that the two cities would unite against their common enemy. In 338 BC the Battle of Charonea decisively demonstrated Macedonian military supremacy and established the Macedonian hegemony of Greece which was to endure for the next two centuries. As master of Greece, Philip was now free to establish the Hellenic League, which he intended to lead against the Persian Empire.

There remained only two major outstanding issues. One was that Sparta remained unconquered and defiant. Philip tried threatening the Spartans by saying 'If I bring my army I will kill your people, destroy your lands and raze your city.' The laconic Spartan reply was 'If.' Since war with Thebes had anyway reduced Sparta to a shadow of its former self, Philip decided that the obdurate Spartans could be safely left alone, and he went on to form his League without them.

The other issue was that Macedonian palace politics remained as lethal as ever. Fully engaged with the diplomatic efforts required to pull the Greeks together for his Persian conquest, Philip took his eye off the ball in this area. During the celebrations which accompanied the marriage of his daughter Cleopatra ('Cleopatra' was a common Macedonian name) Philip ordered his bodyguard to stand well back. He did not want to seem unapproachable to the many foreign and Greek diplomats attending the occasion. This presented a personal enemy with an opportunity. Before his bodyguards could intervene, Philip was stabbed to death before a horrified crowd. The assassin was promptly caught and slain, though many suspected that Philip's wife Olympias was ultimately behind the killing. Philip and Olympias had a turbulent relationship, and Olympias knew that the death of Philip would bring her son Alexander to the throne. And so it came about. In 336 BC, Alexander III became king of Macedon. The army, political alliances and money necessary to undertake the already-planned conquest of Persia were immediately available. All Alexander needed was the will and ability to use the tools that Philip had placed at his disposal.

Persia

The Persian Empire was not an empire of Persians. The Persian heartlands were actually only a small part of literally hundreds of different tribes and cultures in the sprawling landmass that comprised the Persian Empire. At the time when Alexander came to power in Macedon, the Persian Empire was ruled by King Darius III, overlord of domains that stretched from Egypt and the shores of the Mediterranean to the banks of the Indus river and the Hindu Kush mountains of Afghanistan.

Civilization was old in the heartlands of this empire – far older than the civilization of Greece, and in some ways still more advanced. (For example slavery was largely banned.) The twin cores of the empire were the ancient homeland of the Persians in what is now Iran, and the even older civilization of Mesopotamia between the Euphrates and Tigris rivers, where Babylon was the principal city.

In the not-too-distant past the dominant cities of the Mesopotamian region had been Assur and Nineveh. These were the metropolitan hubs of the brutal and repressive Assyrian empire which had dominated the Babylonians, Persians and many other nations beside. When dynastic feuding caused the Assyrians to be weakened by civil war, the Babylonians and Persians took the opportunity to attack the Assyrians. The Assyrian empire was utterly destroyed and Assur and Nineveh were never again more than piles of rubble.

The liberation of the Persians was short-lived, for the nation soon fell under the dominance of a related people – the Medes. It was only in 550 BC that the Persians rose to dominance under the military and political genius of their leader, Cyrus the Great. Cyrus (559–530 BC) well deserves his appellation as the Great, for he not only overthrew the Median empire, but went on, through a mixture of diplomacy and military force, to build the largest empire the world had yet known.

Cyrus seems to have taken to heart the lessons from the fall and destruction of Assyria's brutal regime. His empire allowed peoples to live under their own laws and rulers. How the citizens of the Persian Empire worshipped and were ruled mattered little so long as these citizens acknowledged the overall suzerainty of the empire. Certainly there were taxes to be paid, and military levies to contribute, but the Persians gave much in return. For a start – and very much unlike the Assyrians – the Persians did not interfere with either the religion or economy of subject states. Secondly, the *pax Persica* allowed an unprecedented degree of trade and economic growth that had previously been hampered by endemic warfare.

This mixture of relative freedom, prosperity and political stability gradually won over the Babylonians – the same people who had continually and ferociously resisted the Assyrians. Even the Jews were relatively acquiescent under Persian rule, and this says a great deal, for even at that early date the Hebrews were notoriously recalcitrant subjects. Cyrus repatriated many Jews who had been exiled to the rivers of Babylon (when the Babylonians had briefly conquered Judea), and Persian religious tolerance allowed the rebuilding of the Temple in Jerusalem.

As might be expected of as sprawling and diverse an empire as that ruled by the Persians, there were continual minor rebellions and border wars. However, only two major conquests never became reconciled to Persian rule. These were the Egyptians and the Greek cities of Asia.

The Egyptians were conquered by Cambyses II, the king who succeeded Cyrus. Cambyses somewhat mismanaged this conquest (though, to be fair, conquering Egypt in any fashion at all was an extremely challenging task due to the nation's geography and the obdurate resistance of its peoples). In the course of his conquest Cambyses deeply offended Egyptian religious sensibilities by killing the sacred Apis bull and by replacing the Pharaoh with a governor. The Pharaoh was not only head of state but also an essential conduit between the Egyptians and their gods. His absence was a constant and humiliating reminder to the Egyptian people that thousands of years of Egypt's existence as an independent state had now ended.

The Greeks were a different proposition. The Greek cities of Asia were a fiercely independent lot, wanting to be free not only of Persian rule but that of anyone at all – and that included their fellow Greeks. These Greek cities presented the Persians with a particular problem. For a start, these were some of the major cities of the Persian Empire. Apart from Babylon and the cities of Mesopotamia, most of the interior of the empire was rural and agricultural, or even pastoral. The Greek cities, like the equally independent-minded cities of Phoenicia in the Levant, were important centres of manufacture and trade. This meant that if a Greek city rebelled against Persian rule – which happened regularly – the Persians could not simply flatten the place without hurting their economy in the process.

The only way to govern an empire as large and diverse as that ruled by the Persians was by extreme decentralization of power. Therefore the empire was divided into regions known as 'satrapies' and, given the light touch of the central government, these were close to autonomous kingdoms. Because of the time it took for messages to travel to and from the Persian capital of Pasargadae things could hardly be otherwise. A rebellion might be several months old before the Persian king could react, so trouble with the Greek cities was usually dealt with by the satrap on the ground. While the loss of even a major Greek city might not greatly affect the empire as a whole it would certainly be felt within a particular satrapy, and reflect badly on the satrap.

It did not help that the Greeks of the mainland took great interest in the well-being of their fellow nationals under Persian rule. The Athenians in particular felt that the Greeks of Asia were members of the same Ionian tribe as themselves, and therefore they took the freedom of the Greek cities of Asia as their particular responsibility. Indeed, one of the long-standing charges against Sparta was that the Spartans were all too willing to trade the freedom of the Greeks of Asia in exchange for Persian support against the Athenians.

The western satraps had a complex relationship with the Greeks – both those under their rule and with the independent Greeks of the mainland. Firstly, as mentioned previously, Greek hoplites made better troops than any available on the eastern Mediterranean seaboard. This mattered because it not only made rebellious Greek cities stubbornly hard to reconquer, but because when mainland Greeks got interested enough in the affairs of Asia Minor they brought over armies that it took enormous trouble to eject. However, that same fighting ability had created a considerable demand for Greek mercenaries. These the satraps hired to keep down rebellious subjects (Egypt was a major market) and to fight in the occasional skirmishes the satraps fought between themselves.

The Greeks also traded with the empire. They channelled goods from the western Mediterranean to the Persians and imported even more from Persia for themselves. War tended to destabilize this profitable arrangement, so the satraps tried to keep the Greek cities in their domains happy by granting them considerable autonomy. They even permitted democracy, though contemporary Greek writers report that the Persians themselves fell about laughing at so ridiculous a concept.

The mainland Greeks were controlled with money. Over a century of warfare had wrought huge destruction to the rural economy of Greece, and many landless men had become mercenaries. Not all of these worked for the Persians. Most were even happier to fight for their fellow Greeks so long as they were well paid for doing so. Therefore when two Greek cities fell out – and they did this all the time – the Persians had merely to decide whom they wanted to win, and then give that city lots of money with which to buy mercenaries. The strategy worked in the Peloponnesian War, when the Persians paid the Spartans to defeat the Athenians, and again in the Corinthian war when the Persians paid the Thebans to defeat the Spartans.

The main Persian coin was the Daric, a high-quality gold coin which was usually stamped on the obverse with the image of an archer. When in the 390s the Spartan king Agesilaus II attacked the Persians in Asia Minor he complained that he was driven back by 'ten thousand archers'. These archers did not attack the Spartans directly, but were stamped on the coins which were paid to the Thebans to create so much trouble for the Spartans on the mainland that they were forced to recall Agesilaus and his army.

For obvious reasons, the Greek historians tended to focus on the interaction of the Persians with themselves and the peoples of the Mediterranean. Though our sources are immensely richer for these interactions it is unlikely that the Persian kings spent all their time worrying about the Greeks. There were, for example, Indian kingdoms on the other side of the empire that were richer, more populous and almost as well armed.

In the late sixth-century BC, Persians had taken advantage of regional strife in the Punjab to annex parts of the Indus area and what is now southern Pakistan. Eventually the Gandhara satrapy became the wealthiest and most populous in the empire. The independent neighbours of this satrapy could bring huge resources of their own to bear against it, and these struggles, largely ignored by Western historians ancient and modern, were as vital a preoccupation to the Persian king as his relationship with the Greeks – if not more so.

Furthermore, while a large decentralized empire worked well for its subject peoples, it created a further problem for the Persian king. That is because someone had to do the governing of outlying regions, and of necessity that governor had to be granted a large degree of autonomy. Autonomous governors with the large military force needed to control bandits and hostile neighbours tended to get dangerous ideas. For example they might wonder about how far they could take their independence, and indeed to consider whether they might not be better at ruling the entire empire than the current holder of the job.

As well as the risk of rebellion by an all-too-autonomous satrap, the king had to worry about his own family. Death by successor was so common in the Achaemenid family that it almost counted as death by natural causes. Artaxerxes III (358–338) is a good example. Originally a satrap, he succeeded to the throne after one brother was executed, another was forced to commit suicide, and a third was murdered. As soon as he came to power Artaxerxes executed all those family members who had survived the previous regime. He died allegedly from poison administered by a treasonous vizier who later tried to poison Darius III. (Darius was forewarned, and forced the vizier to drink his own potion.)

These problems with government were highly significant for the later Hellenistic kingdom of Seleucia, because the Seleucids more or less adopted intact the Persian form of government. Consequently they inherited rather the same set of problems, and their inability to find a solution was eventually to destroy their empire.

Egypt

Civilization in Egypt had been long established before the arrival of the Persians. Some of the earliest buildings ever discovered by archaeology are Egyptian, constructed over 6,000 years ago. A good way to grasp the antiquity of Egypt's civilization is to look at the calendar which was established soon after the kingdoms of the Upper and lower Nile were united around 3100 BC.

Like the modern calendar, this had 12 months and 365 days. Unlike the modern calendar, the Egyptian version did not include a leap year. This meant that the calendar fell behind the solar year by one day every four years. To the average Egyptian this did not matter a great deal, since even a long lifetime saw a slippage of only a few days. Yet so old was Egypt that by our period the one day lost every four years had cycled all the way through the calendar – twice. In other words that one day lost every four years had amounted to more than two full years by our period.

When the heirs of Alexander saw the pyramids at Giza these were already middle-aged, half as old as they are now today. Egypt was ancient, and for all those thousands of years it had been an independent nation – until the Persians arrived.

Cambyses II, the Persian king, defeated the Pharaoh Psamtik III in 525 BC and took over the country. Egypt became a satrapy of the Persian

Empire, joined with Phoenicia and Cyprus. That the Egyptians were unhappy with this arrangement was demonstrated four years later when the populace rose in rebellion under a native leader whom they declared to be their new Pharaoh. The Persian Empire was by then ruled by Darius I who suppressed the revolt and then went to great lengths to reconcile the Egyptians to his rule.

This kept the Egyptians quiet until the death of Darius in 486 BC, which prompted another rebellion. Both Persians and Egyptians were getting used to the idea that there would be at least one Egyptian uprising every generation, so no-one was surprised when the next one came right on schedule in 460 BC. This rebellion had the interesting feature that the anti-Persian rebels received substantial aid from the Athenians. After that Egypt was quiet until around 410 BC.

When that long-repressed rebellion came, it was a major affair that mostly drove the Persians from Egypt and allowed the people to declare a precarious independence. The Persians were not entirely expelled. They hung on in some parts of Egypt and in 358 BC a major effort by Persia's new King Artaxerxes reclaimed much of the Nile Valley for fifteen years. It is unknown how this struggle between nationalist sentiment and imperial power would have played out under Darius III. At this point a new player entered the game and Alexander and his successors changed Egypt forever.

The change made by the Greek presence in Egypt was not to the fundamental infrastructure of the country but – as elsewhere in the Hellenistic East – the addition of a new layer of society and culture. The basics of Egyptian life went on as before because climate and geography dictated that this could hardly be otherwise.

The society and geography of Egypt are later explained in detail. For the present all that is needed is an outline to aid with that explanation. For a start, Westerners accustomed by modern cartography to think of north as 'up' need to turn that concept on its head. Egyptian life was based upon the Nile. For the Egyptians 'up' was 'upriver', or south. Therefore the further reaches of the Nile – from Memphis to the southern outpost of Elephantine – were Upper Egypt.

Lower Egypt was the lands of the Nile delta where that great river meets the Mediterranean, and where Egyptian culture met that of other peoples. The Greeks and Phoenicians had long had a presence in Lower Egypt and it was here that the Greek presence was most felt in later centuries. In southern Egypt life under Alexander and his successors mostly went on as it had under the Persians, and before that under the native pharaohs. Every year, the seasonal flooding of the Nile brought with it rich deposits of silt which flooded fields carefully prepared for that event. The rich crops produced by this regular inundation were the foundation of Egyptian wealth and power. Neither Persians nor Greeks (nor later, the Romans) substantially changed either the methods of harvesting or the lives of the peasants who did it.

Away from the 'black lands' alongside the Nile were the 'red lands' of the desert. Apart from the occasional oasis, this was largely uninhabited wilderness until the Egyptians learned to exploit its natural resources. Granite provided material for extensive building projects, and copper deposits helped to make Egypt an international power during the Bronze Age. Alabaster and gold were traded with foreign merchants in Lower Egypt to provide timber and other essentials which the kingdom lacked.

Finally, the desert provided Egypt with defences superior to any city walls. Enemies beyond the southernmost cataracts of the Nile regularly troubled Egypt's rulers, but invasion from east or west was unthinkable. No army could get through the deserts of the west or the barren mountains to the east. The Nile delta was vulnerable to attack from the sea, but the marshy and broken terrain made a poor beachhead. Otherwise, access to Egypt was limited to Gaza. This made that narrow strip of land a constant preoccupation for Egypt's rulers, and until the Roman era no part of the ancient world saw quite as much warfare.

The roots of Hellenism

These three places – tiny Macedon, the sprawling Persian Empire and ancient Egypt – had very little in common. Macedon was tightly centralized, Egypt largely ruled through a priestly aristocracy, and the Persian Empire was a patchwork of tribal federations, independent cities and individual kingdoms (not for nothing was the Persian ruler entitled 'the King of Kings'). The culture of each state was different, the societies were alien to one another, and each worshipped very different gods. How then was Hellenism able to put down roots and become established in such unwelcoming soil?

The answer lies in the culture of the southern Greek states. The Greeks had developed the autonomous city-state into almost an art form. Long before Alexander the Greeks had exported the end product across the known world. There were dozens of Greek city states in mainland Greece, but there were well over a hundred more scattered across the Mediterranean world, from the shores of the Black Sea (which the Greeks called the Euxine) to the Strait of Gibraltar in the west ('the Pillars of Hercules').

From the borders of Phoenicia northwards, Greek cities dotted the coastline of Asia Minor. The cities of Mytilene, Halicarnassus and Ephesus had produced respectively the poet Sappho, the historian Herodotus and the Temple of Artemis, one of the seven wonders of the ancient world. No-one doubted that these cities were totally Greek. Yet each thrived away from the Greek mainland, and in the case of Halicarnassus, Ephesus and many, many more the hinterland of each city belonged to a very different culture to the urban Greeks.

Greek culture was well established in the cities of Sicily and southern Italy. Roman culture developed as it did through the Greek-influenced Etruscans and with direct interaction with Greek colonies such as Tarentum and Naples ('Naples' in the original Greek meant 'New city' – *nea polis*). By the time the armies of Alexander were ready to explode across Mesopotamia and points further east, the Hellenistic city had become an ideal vehicle for making the new conquests durable. By 336 BC, there was a long-established formula for the process of taking Greek settlers, dropping them into an alien environment and ending up with yet another island of Greek culture.

Whether on the eastern coast of Iberia or the western slopes of the Himalayas, settlers in the newly-founded Hellenistic cities expected to exercise in the gymnasium, sacrifice to the Olympian gods in classic Greek temples, and in the theatre watch the same plays that their contemporaries were enjoying thousands of miles away.

What the native peoples were expected to make of the Greek city which had landed in their midst did not seem to concern the settlers much. Certainly there was no organized effort to 'civilize' these peoples into a Greek way of life. If native peoples adopted aspects of Greek culture, the initiative came from below. What the Greeks asked of the peoples in the lands where they settled was that they remain peaceful and provide raw materials for manufacture and trade. Whether these people were Egyptian, Italian or Babylonian mattered little. With one major exception – which we shall come to later – the Greeks of the Hellenistic kingdoms remained Greek.

Chapter 2

Alexander Conquers the World (Part I)

Greek though the Macedonians might now officially be, Alexander was still very much a Macedonian king. Unlike some leaders to the south, one did not become king of Macedon through charm and a winning personality, and one certainly did not remain king that way. Macedonian kings survived – to the extent they survived at all – by being ruthless, decisive and very paranoid. The attrition rate among Alexander's immediate predecessors demonstrated that, even so, the regular vacancies for the Macedonian throne occurred because the previous occupant had not been paranoid and merciless enough.

It is important to remember this, because the glory of his conquests rather blinded later Greek and Roman writers to some aspects of Alexander's character. There is a tendency to bestow a certain nobility on a man who was ultimately a ruthless conqueror and an unromantic practitioner of realpolitik. We should also note that Alexander was seldom sober enough to constitute a good role model for anyone but Attila the Hun.

Like his father before him, Alexander was polygamous. Alexander's mother, the redoubtable Olympias, was but one of several wives whom Philip picked up in the course of diplomatic marriages. We get a flavour of life at the royal court on the occasion when Philip married yet another wife. This was Eurydice, the niece of Philip's general Attalus.

Attalus, well drunk, proposed a toast with hopes to the effect that the niece's marriage would produce a legitimate heir to the Macedonian kingdom. This resulted in an infuriated Alexander hurling a wine-cup at Attalus' head. 'What! Are you calling me a bastard?'

Philip sided with Attalus and in his reckless rage he might have stabbed his son. But he was so drunk that – by good fortune – his foot slipped and he planted his face on the floor. Standing over him

Alexander proclaimed 'Take a look. The man who proposes to leap from Europe to Asia can't even spring from couch to couch.'

(from Plutarch, *Alexander*, 9)

Once Alexander came to power Attalus was promptly murdered. Alexander's vindictive mother went even further. 'Olympias killed Eurydice, niece of Attalus [and Eurydice's] and Philip's infant son by pulling them over a red-hot bronze urn', reports the later writer Pausanias (8.7.5). House-cleaning continued with the killing of Alexander's cousin Amyntas IV – the supposed king for whom Philip had begun his career as regent. Two other young rivals for the throne were disposed of at the same time.

Having got started by cowing the Macedonian court into a proper state of abject terror, Alexander found that he had to do the same to the rest of the world. As soon as Philip was murdered, the peace he had made with the northern barbarians became null and void. At once the barbarians rose and launched an assault on the Macedonian heartlands. Noting that Macedon had changed rulers and immediately developed barbarian problems, the leading states of southern Greece (ie Athens and Thebes) promptly repudiated the Macedonian overlordship which Philip had imposed.

According to Plutarch, Alexander's advisers recommended abandoning Macedon's hold on Greece and making whatever terms they could with the barbarian invaders. Then, with the immediate crisis over, Alexander could secure his position on the throne and rebuild from there. Alexander took a contrary view. If he showed weakness now, his enemies would be all over him.

In any case, Philip had left to Alexander the compact but potent army which was to be the spearhead of the invasion of Persia. Alexander was more than ready to put this army through its paces by exercising it against the kingdom's foreign enemies. Consequently the startled barbarians found themselves dealing with a Macedonian counter-invasion which took Alexander as far as the Danube. When the leader of the barbarian confederacy, one King Syrmus, rallied his people in defence of their homeland, Alexander's army crushed them in battle.

This eliminated the barbarian threat and thereafter it was with a somewhat more experienced army that Alexander turned south. The Thebans were defiant, which proved a mistake. Rather as he had with the northern barbarians, Alexander had a point to make. When the Thebans rudely rejected the mild peace terms which he offered, Alexander unleashed his army on the city. Thebes was captured, plundered and the remains were burned to the ground. What had been the mightiest city in Greece just a generation before was converted to a pile of smoking rubble. After separating out the few pro-Macedonian citizens in their midst, Alexander sold the remaining Thebans into slavery – some 30,000 of them. There were attempts to rebuild and repopulate Thebes in later years, but the city never recovered. Today it is a town of some 25,000 people.

The object lesson was not lost on the Athenians. Fortunately Alexander wanted Greece as partners in his Persian invasion, and he could hardly achieve that by demolishing its cities. Therefore he and the Athenians set about mollifying each other. Alexander even went so far as to spare Demosthenes. The great Athenian orator had been violently anti-Macedonian from the start and had launched a series of scathing attacks on the Macedonian monarchy in speeches which are known today as *The Philippics*. Demosthenes had also received (and allegedly embezzled) a very large sum of gold from Darius III which was intended as a Persian subsidy for a Greek rebellion against Alexander.

Alexander's gentle treatment of Athens was the velvet glove wrapped around the iron fist which had destroyed Thebes. The combination was persuasive enough to bring all the southern Greek states back into the Hellenic alliance, with the recalcitrant Spartans being – as ever – the only exception. Alexander now had prepared his ground. Enemies foreign and domestic were cowed, his army was experienced and raring to go. It was now or never, especially as Macedon – never a rich country – could not remain at this level of preparedness for long before the money ran out. As it was the Persian invasion was an all-or-nothing gamble by Alexander. To raise funds and win over supporters he had mortgaged and given away so much of the royal estates in Macedon that if the invasion failed he would have almost nothing to return home to.

The expedition which would change the world was launched in the spring of 334 BC. The core of Alexander's army was the phalanx of 12,000 Macedonians, men who were at that time probably the finest infantry in the known world. These were supported by 1,800 of Alexander's Companion cavalry – another elite unit. This Macedonian element made up about half of the Hellenic army. The remainder were either Greek contingents from the Hellenic League or mercenaries which some cities had sent in lieu of their own citizens. A smattering of barbarians such as Illyrians and Thracians were added to the mix, either because of treaty obligations or because some volunteers scented the possibility of booty. Overall, the invasion force consisted of around 30,000 infantry, 5,000 cavalry and around 2,000 specialist troops such as skirmishers and archers.

This was not a large army with which to attack an empire as large as that of the Persians. A century and a half previously, when Xerxes I was going the other way to conquer Greece, he took an army estimated at 300,000 men. That's ten times the size of Alexander's army, and includes a substantial discount in numbers to allow for the exaggerations of Greek historians.

To balance this huge disparity in numbers, Alexander was counting on two factors. The first was the inertia which was inevitably built into any empire as large as that of Darius III. Organizing and mustering an army with levies from outlying regions took time, and there was the matter of carefully organizing the troops and their commanders to ensure that the new army's first move was not to turn on Darius III and set up the Persian Empire under new management. Even in the Anatolian satrapies directly affected by Alexander's army, there was confusion and debate among the Persian governors instead of an organized response to the invasion.

Secondly, though Alexander's army was a great deal smaller than its Persian counterpart, it was also a great deal better. Both sides were well aware of this fact, which had been proven repeatedly over two centuries of warfare. The Persian armies were mainly bowmen backed by an assortment of cavalry which ranged from horse archers to heavily-armoured aristocrats on horseback. It was an army which had evolved to deal with the open and arid conditions of the Iranian plateau and points east, and it was very good at what it did. Unfortunately for Darius and his satraps, what it could not do was fight Greek pikemen, for the army lacked a component of experienced heavy infantry capable of going toe-to-toe with Alexander's phalanx.

Consequently, Darius' defence against Alexander in the major battles consisted of a series of attempts to force battle in conditions which nullified the Macedonian advantage in infantry. This was essential because while Persian armies might be massive, they were also fragile. Most of those in the Persian ranks were levies drawn from parts of the empire unaffected by Alexander's invasion and none too enamoured of Persian rule to begin with. Apart from a hard core of very good Persian troops, none of the remainder of the army considered the defence of the Persian Empire a cause worth dying for – and repeated experience at fighting the Greeks suggested that dying was very much a possibility.

While the Persian strategy focussed on nullifying the Greek phalanx, Alexander's strategy was to ram his small army into the Persian ranks and break the enemy apart. The best way to do this was to use the phalanx to pin the mass of the enemy army while Alexander and his Companion cavalry looked for a chance to hit the enemy somewhere vulnerable. In every battle apart from the Granicus such a killing stroke by the Macedonian cavalry was essential lest the Persians otherwise eventually overwhelm Alexander's army by sheer force of numbers.

The first test came a month after Alexander's invasion force left Greece. The Persian satraps mustered a scratch army against the invaders and took up a defensive position on the banks of the River Granicus. In doing this they were being both cautious and rash. The regional satraps ignored advice to retreat before the Greek invasion, stripping the land of supplies as they went. The superior numbers of the Persian cavalry could stop extensive foraging by the Macedonians, so by the time that Alexander had advanced far inland his army would be hungry and demoralized, vulnerable to Darius and his army when he arrived in overwhelming force.

Thus, given that this option was available – and strongly proposed by the leader of the Greek mercenaries in Persian employ – the decision to make a stand against the invaders was rash. However, if the satraps were going to be rash, they intended to be rash as cautiously as possible. The position they chose was on a major route near the city of Dascylium (Ergili in modern Turkey) on high ground overlooking the River Granicus at a point where the terrain would channel the enemy into confined space which limited manoeuvre.

We are fortunate to have an account of the battle from Alexander's biographer, Arrian, and yet another account by the historian Diodorus Siculus. We are unfortunate in that these two accounts differ to the extent that they largely describe two different battles. However, by taking the points that these two histories have in common, a general picture emerges.

The Persians had rightly decided that the best counter to Greek infantry was Greek infantry. Therefore they had an army of some 19,000 Greek mercenaries drawn up in support of the cavalry. The cavalry was intended to be the striking arm which would hit the Macedonians in force while they were still disorganized from crossing the river.

The plan was good, the execution poor. What the Persians had forgotten was that Alexander had a compact, well-trained army that had lately been practising a lot more than usual. The expectation was that when Alexander saw the massed ranks of the enemy mustered against him, he would stop and take stock before deploying. Instead his army launched a quick cavalry feint on one flank and then pushed right on across the river. By the time the Persians had realized what was happening and got their cavalry organized, it was too late – the Macedonians were across and in battle order.

By this reckoning, the battle was won by the slick speed and professionalism of the Macedonian army. Early in the proceedings Alexander made a sudden move sideways with a section of his troops. The point of this move has baffled later military historians, but more to the point it probably also baffled the Persians who were scrambling to get their act together in any case.

The end result was rather similar to a bar fight in which one man gets punched on the chin before he is properly aware that the fight has even started. The Persians were still in the fight, but they never got over that initial setback. Cavalry are somewhat useless against formed infantry, and even more so against pikes, so the next job of the Persian commanders was to clear their massed cavalry from the front of the Macedonian phalanx as it marched purposefully uphill.

The object was to get the Persian horse out of the way in a hurry before it was trapped against the mercenaries who made up the Persian infantry. The cavalry escaped the jaws of the infantry vice, but squirted out of the sides of the closing battle lines in some disorder. At this point the Macedonian cavalry fell upon them, killed their commanders and chased the rest from the field. The heaviest fighting occurred at this point, and Alexander was in the thick of it. At one point he would have been killed had not one of his companions – Black Cleitus – lopped the arm off the man about to stab his king.

Once the Persian cavalry had been driven back, there was nothing to protect the flanks and rear of the Persian infantry contingent. The light skirmishers of the Persian army made a quick assessment of how the battle was going and joined their cavalry in a high-speed retreat. The infantry had no such option. If the Greek mercenaries broke ranks and ran, the Macedonian cavalry would massacre them. If they kept formation they would be outnumbered, surrounded and cut down.

The mercenaries attempted to negotiate, but they had nothing to offer. Alexander would take nothing less than complete and unconditional surrender, and eventually that is what he got. Surrender did not save the lives of half the mercenaries who were executed anyway. The others were enslaved and shipped back to Greece. Overall, Alexander lost around 400 men, while the Persians probably lost ten times that number.

(There are other hypotheses as to what happened in this confusing battle. There is a good discussion of alternative views by N G L Hammond in *The Journal of Hellenic Studies*, vol 100 1980, pp 73–88, 'The battle of the Granicus River'.)

The Persian casualties do not include the loss of the Greek mercenaries who perished after the battle was over. In his merciless treatment of fellow Greeks Alexander was not simply being tyrannical for the sake of it. As his treatment of Thebes had earlier demonstrated, Alexander had no problem with object lessons written in blood. In this case he wanted to say – in the clearest possible terms – that Greeks fighting for the Persians was unacceptable. This was not only because Greeks fighting on the other side diluted the message of a Hellenic crusade, but because Greek mercenaries represented almost the only decent heavy infantry that the Persians could put in the field. By terminally discouraging the enrolment of such mercenaries Alexander attempted to deprive the Persians of an essential component of any army that could stop him.

To reaffirm the status of his invasion as a pan-Hellenic enterprise, Alexander sent captured armour back to Athens to be given as trophies to Athena. The effect was rather spoiled because even in his moment of triumph Alexander could not resist a cheap shot. The accompanying inscription to the trophies read 'Taken from the barbarians of Asia by Alexander, son of Philip together with all the Greeks – except the Spartans.'

The satraps' gamble had failed. The price of that failed gamble was more severe than the loss of heavy infantry – severe though that loss indeed was. Along with victory at the Granicus, Alexander took possession of most of western Anatolia, and the cities and revenues thereof. A campaign that had until now been struggling for funds was now flush with cash. An immediate fill-up of booty accompanied by the certainty of regular pay in future did much to further boost the morale of a Greek army already elated by victory. Furthermore, those Anatolian cities and tribes which had been awaiting the result of that first clash before declaring their unconditional allegiance to the Persian king now declined to do so altogether, moving yet more of Asia Minor out of Persian control.

Alexander was to win many more major victories, but in many ways the Battle of the River Granicus was the most important. Defeat in subsequent battles would have set Alexander back, but only at the Granicus would a defeat have finished him.

For a while after the Granicus, Alexander faced no major opposition and spent the rest of the year consolidating his grip on Asia Minor. Persian garrisons were ejected from Greek and native cities up and down the western seaboard, an operation partly designed to deprive the Persian navy of bases from which it could strike at Alexander's lines of communication with Greece. In a significant move, when the major city of Halicarnassus fell into his power, Alexander did not transfer the control of the city to a subordinate but instead left it in the hands of the ruling dynasty. This marked the beginning of a process by which Alexander was to slowly transition from being king of Macedon to King of Asia – a change which caused some consternation and dismay among his followers.

That Alexander was keen to become 'King of Asia' was shown when his army reached the city of Gordium in the inland state of Phrygia. The city was proud of a massively complex knot which tradition claimed could only be loosed by someone with the coveted title. Alexander's direct solution has become proverbial. He cut through the Gordian knot.

At this point the campaign paused for a moment. Alexander was struggling with illness, and doubtless Persian spies observed that without Alexander, the entire Greek army ground to a halt. Alexander seems to have come to the same conclusion about Darius, who was now coming up fast with a substantial force. Take out Darius, and you took out his army. The struggle between the two kings became personal.

This was clearly demonstrated at the first clash of kings, which happened late in the year 333 BC near the little town of Issus in southern Asia Minor. Through some confused pre-battle manoeuvring, Darius managed to place himself and an army some 80,000 strong across Alexander's lines of communication. In the process Darius cut himself off from his own supply lines, a combination of circumstances which made battle inevitable. (Greek historians put Darius' army at a quarter of a million and upwards, a number which is simply unfeasible given the time of year and the logistical issues involved. While 80,000 is a reasonable estimate, the number may have been as high as 100,000. Either way, Alexander was substantially outnumbered.)

Darius had ended in a generally favourable position on the northern bank of the Pinarus River, rather similar to the position that the Persians had occupied at the Granicus, with the major difference being that the Persian right flank was anchored by the Gulf of Issus, and the left on the foothills of the Amanus range. This slightly cramped battleground meant that the Persians could not extend their lines to outflank the Greeks, but on the other hand they could deploy in depth. Since the Greeks would have to cut through the Persian army to restore its line of communication this was no bad thing.

Darius may have been made even more confident because this time the Persian army had decent heavy infantry. This consisted of the 10,000 Persian 'Immortals' who made up the core of any Royal Persian army, and around 10,000 Greek mercenaries who had not yet got Alexander's message. This meant that the Persians had heavy infantry at least as numerous as Alexander's phalanx and twice the cavalry. The cavalry were extremely good, which is more than can be said for the native levies of light infantry who made up the rest of the army. The relatively tight confines of the coastal plain where the battle was fought made these infantry somewhat superfluous in any case.

Persian cavalry superiority was decisive in the early stages of the battle when the Persians crossed the river and confidently engaged the weaker horse commanded by Alexander's trusted subordinate Parmenio. The Greek mercenaries deployed alongside the Persian cavalry were also able to hold their own against Alexander's phalanx. This meant that with Parmenio's cavalry slowly giving way, the Macedonians were in danger of eventually being outflanked.

One reason for the Persian success on their right flank was that Alexander had focussed his strength on the other side of the battle line, the side where the Persian king had stationed himself. Alexander's infantry attacked across the river and, despite this disadvantage, the veteran Macedonian troops were able to create a temporary gap in the Persian battle line. This gap presented Alexander with the opportunity he had been seeking. At the head of his Companion cavalry Alexander plunged into the midst of the Persian army and made straight for the Persian king. The sight of a homicidal Alexander cutting through the ranks toward him was too much for Darius. Wheeling his chariot about, he left the battlefield in a hurry.

The prospect of cutting down the Great King and taking over the Persian Empire at a stroke must have tempted Alexander. But most of the Persian army had not yet realized that their king had abandoned them, and the rest of the Greek army was in trouble. Alexander had to choose – pursue Darius and win the empire, or fall on the rear of the Greek mercenary phalanx (which had now moved forward past Alexander's own advance) and win the battle?

With typical decisiveness, Alexander unhesitatingly chose the latter option. As the mercenary phalanx splintered, it dawned on the rest of the Persian army that their king was not around to rally them. The Persian army quickly dissolved into a crowd of panicked individuals all with a major interest in being elsewhere as soon as possible. For many this was not possible at all, for Alexander followed up his victory methodically and ruthlessly, killing the enemy in huge numbers as they fled the battlefield. The only mercy he showed was to the womenfolk of Darius' family who had accompanied the king with the royal court.

Thus, at Issus, not only did southern Asia Minor fall to Alexander's arms, but so did Darius' mother, wife and daughters (one of whom Alexander later married). Just as importantly, Alexander took possession of Darius' war chest and the huge financial reserves which backed the Persian field army. Within two years Alexander had transformed himself from the cash-strapped leader of a small mountain kingdom to the extremely wealthy overlord of Asia Minor. And he was just getting started.

Darius was informed of this in no uncertain terms when he offered a peace deal after Issus. The Persian king offered to surrender to Alexander the lands he had already conquered, plus a massive ransom for his captured family members. Alexander's general Parmenio is said to have remarked that it was a good deal. 'I would take that offer if I were you, Alexander.' Alexander replied, 'Indeed I would – if I were Parmenio.' He then sent a reply to Darius to say that it was he who would make the terms of who could keep what lands and pay what ransom. In effect he was saying that it was he, Alexander, who was now master of the Persian Empire – Darius had just not realized it yet.

The invasion of the south

Having secured Anatolia, it might have seemed logical for Alexander to follow up the victory at Issus by driving for Mesopotamia and securing the heartlands of the Persian Empire. After all, it was a good idea to do this before Darius could raise both another army and the morale of his dejected followers. Instead Alexander took the calculated gamble of allowing his opponent breathing space while he turned his attention to the Levant and the rest of the Mediterranean seaboard.

This was not an obvious step. Given Alexander's boundless self-confidence we can assume that he intended from the start to conquer Syria, Palestine and Egypt. The question is why did he want to do it just then? If Persia was defeated then the subject states might drop into Alexander's hands without a fight. With Persia undefeated, Alexander might expect at least token resistance from the garrisons and satraps Darius had ruling that part of the empire. Secondly, conquered lands had to be kept under Macedonian control, which meant that troops and competent subordinate commanders had to be diverted from the main army for this task – at a time when that main army was yet to face the challenge of meeting Darius in the heartlands of the empire.

These matters would have been discussed by Alexander and his generals in council before any decision was taken. It was usual for a Hellenistic king to consult with his advisors before making any major moves, but in the end the decision rested with him. Afterwards Alexander decided that before attacking Persia it was essential to secure the Mediterranean seaboard. He was probably right. For a start the Persian navy was a threat. This navy was largely crewed by Pontic and Phoenician sailors, and both nations produced competent seamen.

Marching inland without neutralizing the Persian navy would leave this threat behind unchecked. Such was the size of the Persian Empire that Persepolis, the capital of Darius' empire, lay over two months march from the Mediterranean coast. Even if his army was marching unopposed and in a hurry Alexander would be far too late to undo any mischief that the Persian fleet might wreak in his absence.

With support from the Persian navy, the island states of Ionia might be encouraged to rebel (the Persian fleet had earlier taken the city of Miletus) and the satrap of Egypt might well be scheming with the Spartans to wrest mainland Greece from Macedonian control. (In fact the Spartans were conspiring directly with Darius himself, but Alexander only discovered that later.)

Alexander was only going to march his small army all the way to the River Tigris when he was certain that the land and sea behind him was secure. Leaving the Levant and Egypt in a position to move north and into Anatolia, Ionia and Greece proper presented an unacceptable risk.

Furthermore, if Alexander did conquer the Persians first, he might arguably make the conquest of the rest of the Persian Empire harder. Were Persia to be crushed militarily then Egypt, Judea, and the Phoenician cities would promptly defect from the empire and reclaim the independence for which they yearned. Egypt might not fight very hard for Darius, but they would fight like tigers to hold on to their newly-regained independence. The same went double for the Jews. Therefore, it was better not to take the freedom of these states after the fall of Persia but instead to simply make them change masters beforehand.

That the peoples of the Levant would not fight hard for the Persians was confirmed as the Macedonian army moved south through Syria and occupied northern Phoenicia without much fuss. The first stumbling block came at Tyre, where the citizens reckoned that they could manage without either the Persians or Macedonians. Tyre was an island at this time (it was later joined to the mainland by a causeway), and had walls that started right against the sea. There was nowhere for Alexander to even establish a beachhead, and the Tyrians reckoned that with so much pressing business elsewhere, Alexander would not be able to afford the time for a lengthy siege.

Militarily, this was probably correct, but the importance of Tyre went beyond this. If Tyre was seen to successfully defy Alexander then every Phoenician city with a halfway defensible position would be tempted to do likewise. On the other hand, if nearly-invulnerable Tyre was crushed for its defiance then resistance elsewhere in the Levant was unlikely. The corpses of the Greek mercenaries and the citizens of Thebes were mute witnesses to Alexander's penchant for horrible examples. Tyre would be another, however long it took.

It took seven months. During this time Alexander would have been acutely aware that Darius was raising and training new levies in Mesopotamia, and the satrap of Egypt was desperately fortifying Gaza against the coming attack. Fortunately for Alexander, his previous conquests meant that Macedonia was for the first time a naval power. Even with an abundance of ships – the Cypriots decided spontaneously to join in and contributed a further naval contingent – breaking Tyre's massive walls with ship-based rams was nevertheless an exasperating and time-consuming process.

Perseverance paid off, and eventually a breach was made in the wall. Immediately the Macedonians attacked in overwhelming force, not only at the point of the breach but also at the harbour and on the opposite side of the city. The intention was to force the defenders to split their forces, and it worked. Eventually the Tyrians were forced to abandon the walls and fight from a strongpoint within the city. But by then the end was inevitable.

As punishment for the city's earlier mistreatment of Alexander's envoys, 2,000 Tyrians were crucified on the beach. Another 6,000 men of military age were killed, though it is not clear whether this was in the fighting or after they had surrendered. The remainder of the population were enslaved, and the rest of Phoenicia was cowed by the subsequent methodical destruction of half the city. Thereafter Alexander faced little resistance until he arrived in Gaza at the entrance to Egypt.

The delay at Tyre had allowed Betis, Persian satrap of Egypt to spend a lot of time fortifying and provisioning the fortress at Gaza. This fortress blocked access to Egypt via Sinai rather as a cork in a bottle. The place was regarded as unassailable, and this gave Alexander all the more incentive to take it. If the famed defences of Tyre and Gaza proved unable to withstand Alexander's armies, then other cities would be prepared to promptly surrender.

Furthermore, unwelcome as the delay had been, the siege of Tyre had produced two benefits. Firstly, there seems little doubt that while Alexander was camped outside Tyre Macedonian agents were busy within Egypt preparing the population for Alexander's arrival. It was stressed that Alexander came as a liberator, not a conqueror. He was prepared to work with the Egyptian people and to respect their customs and their gods. The Macedonian message found a receptive audience. Egypt was prepared to welcome Alexander – if he could get past Gaza.

A second consequence of the siege of Tyre was that Alexander now had at hand a large array of siege weaponry, from rams to towers to artillery. Despite this abundance of weaponry to throw at the task, the attack on Gaza proved hard work. The Macedonians were thrown back three times and Alexander himself suffered an injured shoulder. Nevertheless, the time and effort put into the investment of Gaza paid off, for when the fortress finally fell to Alexander, Egypt fell also.

Gaza itself became Ghastly Object Lesson Number Four, with the adult male population slain and the women and children sold into slavery. Betis himself was killed – horribly.

While still alive he was tied by cords from his ankles to the king's chariot. The horses dragged him around the city and Alexander bragged that he, the descendant of Achilles, had destroyed an enemy in a like manner.

(from Quintus Curtius, *History of Alexander,* 4.6.8 – Achilles had dragged the body of Hector around the walls of Troy.)

The horrible example sufficed. Alexander's advance into Egypt was more of a triumphal procession than a military campaign. Alexander showed his deference to the Egyptian gods by visiting the sacred bull of Ra-Amun at the ancient Oasis at Siwa. In return the oracle informed Alexander that Zeus himself was his true father, and not Philip II. (Philip's widow Olympias had been saying the same thing for some time, but it was only after divine confirmation at Siwa that Alexander made the claim official.)

Alexander was only in Egypt for a few months, but his visit left an indelible mark on the country. This is because Alexander immediately set about establishing a Greek-style city on Egypt's Mediterranean coast, a city intended to balance the power of the ancient Egyptian cities along the Nile. His chosen site (as the consequence of a dream, says the biographer Plutarch) was on the Canoptic branch of the Nile at the small port of Rhakotis, a town already over a millennium old. Alexander himself had pressing business elsewhere, so, after preparing the basic layout and formally founding the city in 331 BC, he left further development to a subordinate called Cleomenes.

The new city was called Alexandria-on-the-Nile. However it totally eclipsed the many other cities around the Middle East which Alexander later named after himself, to the point where this city became simply 'Alexandria' – and it remains so called today. Alexandria under Cleomenes was nothing like the major metropolis it was to become, but Cleomenes did his bit by getting the infant city off to a good start.

The city was designed from the beginning with wide streets carefully angled to catch the prevailing breezes. Generous allocation was made for administrative and other civic buildings, and the port facilities of little Rhakotis were massively enlarged. Either Alexander or a subordinate with a good understanding of economics had quickly grasped that the destruction of Tyre had left a hole in the web of trading ports which bound together the Mediterranean economy. The new city of Alexandria was aggressively promoted both as a replacement for Tyre and as a gateway to the wealth of the Egyptian interior. The city flourished from the start, and was to go on to become one of the greatest capitals of the ancient world.

The Camel's Hump, 331 BC

Egypt was captured, and Syria and the Levant secure. Now the final reckoning with Darius awaited. Alexander began by dallying in Asia Minor in the hope that Darius would come to him. (He was also expecting reinforcements from Greece which never arrived due to domestic troubles.) Eventually, realizing that Darius would not be drawn, and that his reinforcements were indefinitely delayed, Alexander led his men on the long march to the Persian interior.

Darius had indeed been preparing an army. Here ancient and modern historians radically disagree. Plutarch, writing around 400 years after the event, opts for a Persian army of 1,000,000 men, presumably because he wanted a nice, large, round number. This figure has been severely pruned by revisionist historians, some of whom allow Darius only a stingy army of some 50,000 men. (cf the review by G L Cawkwell in *The Classical Review*, Vol. 15, No. 2 (Jun., 1965), pp. 203–205.)

In one way, the size of the Persian army is not strictly relevant. The army was not gathered for a campaign where its different components might outmanoeuvre an enemy, or for a war of conquest where garrisons would need to be hived off to control different areas as they fell under the army's control. Under these circumstances, a large – and preferably well-trained – army was very useful. This was not the case with the Persians. Darius had opted for a single all-or-nothing confrontation. Perhaps this was because he did not trust either the loyalty or the training of his levies and he feared that they might either defect or that Alexander would be able to defeat them piecemeal. Perhaps he did indeed only have 50,000 men.

Even if Darius had 500,000 men most of that army would be superfluous. Alexander had around 50,000 men and such was the nature of combat in ancient warfare that fighting happened mostly one-on-one, whether the 'one' was a single combatant or an infantry unit. While that was going on there was no space for the other members of the outnumbering side to participate without getting in the way. They had to wait their turn.

By this argument the battle becomes a much more evenly balanced affair. Many of the levies that Darius had summoned to the battle were relatively light-armed troops. Alexander's well armoured, close-packed and highly motivated phalanx could roll over any such unit without breaking a sweat, and the unit after that, and the one after that until Darius' numerical advantage was gone. Therefore, the significant troops on the Persian side were Darius' 10,000 Immortals and 2 – 8,000 Greek mercenaries who could, after Alexander's earlier treatment of their colleagues, be counted on to fight to the death. The rest of the infantry were essentially window-dressing.

Cavalry were a different matter. The open frontiers to the east required the Persians to have a large, diverse and competent cavalry force. Consequently, the cavalry had Cappadocian javelinmen, Scythian horse archers and heavy cavalry, armoured horsemen from Parthia and Persia and even a camel-mounted contingent from Bactria.

Darius and his advisors had given considerable thought as to where they were going to put this army. A competent Persian commander had successfully blockaded approaches along the Euphrates, leaving Alexander little choice but to strike for the Tigris across northern Assyria. Darius intended to meet him on a plain near the city of Arbela. This was dominated by a low hill shaped like a camel's hump and it is from the Hellenization of the native term for this hump – *gammelu* – that the Battle of Gaugamela gets its name.

At Gaugamela the Persians worked hard to overcome the factors which had led to defeat at Issus and the Granicus. This time the terrain was open, so the superior Persian cavalry would have room to manoeuvre. To counter the pikes of the Macedonian phalanx the Persians had prepared some 200 heavy chariots with large scythes fitted to the wheels. These chariots moving at speed could hit vulnerable infantry rather in the manner that a hand blender hits a fruit salad. However, getting the chariots to be effective required the exact management of their deployment in precisely the right circumstances – which is the reason why scythe chariots feature so seldom in ancient warfare and are generally unsuccessful when they do. Darius had done what he could by making sure the ground was smoothed out, and that his chariots would have a smooth line of approach.

The battle started propitiously for Alexander – literally. The night before the fatal engagement the moon turned blood-red and then vanished completely. By the most optimistic interpretation this eclipse signalled a major setback for Persia, but Jupiter was not visible and Saturn was. This planetary alignment caused the worried Babylonian astrologers to observe that the stars predicted complete and utter disaster for the Persians. Consequently, the Persians – who had already been defeated by Alexander in Gaza, and at the Granicus and Issus – did not muster for battle in the best of spirits.

Alexander started the battle by attacking on the right with his cavalry. Darius threw cavalry out even further on that flank to push the Macedonians back and so prevent the battle straying from the killing field which he had prepared for his scythed chariots. In fact, with Alexander's cavalry partly screening his infantry as the struggle on the right flank became more intense, this seemed a good moment to unleash the aforesaid chariots.

It turned out that the chariots were expected. Light horse immediately deployed to take out the charioteers with javelins, and those chariots that reached the infantry lines found that the phalanx smoothly opened into lanes down which the chariots charged ineffectually. As the chariots wheeled to re-engage behind the infantry, they were dispatched by light troops deployed for just that purpose.

Again, this shows that, without getting any explicit mention by contemporary historians, Alexander's espionage was hard-working and effective. Troops in a tight-packed phalanx can't engage in impromptu drills on the fly without collapsing into chaos. Nor was it coincidence that the right troops to take out the chariots were in the right place at the right time. The army nullified the threat with the ease that only practice and preparation can achieve, which suggests that Alexander was reliably informed of what he was facing well ahead of time.

Nevertheless, the battle was going Darius' way. His superior cavalry were on the way to getting Alexander's horse pinned against the phalanx, and the light infantry – useless in a head-on clash – were advancing at a rate which would eventually take them around to the Macedonian rear. All the Immortals had to do was pin Alexander's phalanx until the light troops got behind it and victory was inevitable. Perhaps those immense numbers could be made to work after all.

Alexander was well aware that his men would eventually be swamped by Persian numbers. His advantage was that unit-for-unit his men were better armed and trained than their adversaries. Therefore he had to use these units in a single do-or-die effort. While the cavalry held off the Persian horse on his right, Alexander organized his cavalry and the infantry on his left into a huge wedge that drove right at the heart of the Persian army, with Alexander and his elite Companion cavalry at the tip of that wedge.

At the heart of the Persian army was Darius. Without the advantage of modern communications he had only an imperfect idea of how the battle was going. He did not know that Alexander had thrown every unit he had available into this single effort. He did not know that the Greek cavalry was slowly buckling and his units on the flanks of Alexander's army were poised to sweep around and envelop the enemy. The cavalry fight raised huge clouds of dust across the plain, and in the confusion messengers often arrived late, with contradictory information and sometimes did not arrive at all. All Darius knew for sure was what he could see – that the ranks immediately before him were crumpling and fleeing, and Macedonian standards were advancing inexorably on his position. For all he knew, the situation was the same right along the battle line.

Darius fled, and Alexander did not pursue. His army was in trouble, and increasingly desperate messages from Parmenio told him that his cavalry could not hold out much longer. With Darius gone, it was now a matter of holding on until the Persian army became aware of his absence. Then, with an enemy which was already half-expecting defeat, Persian morale would collapse. Which is what developed, though the fact that the Persian cavalry broke through the Macedonian lines and got as far as Alexander's camp shows that Alexander's charge came not a moment too soon. Any later, and Alexander might have taken the king but lost his army.

As it was, most of the Persian levies had not wanted to be there in the first place, were demoralized by the omens before the battle and by a history of defeat at Alexander's hands. They knew as little about what was going on as anyone else and reasonably decided that if anyone was on top of the situation, it was their king. So if Darius had given up the battle as a lost cause, there was little point in sticking around to be massacred by a Macedonian army that had a proven taste for slaughter.

The Persian army dispersed at high speed, and the army that collapsed at Gaugamela that twentieth day of September 331 BC took the Persian Empire down with it. There was a lot still to do, and many of Darius' domains were still under his control, but after Gaugamela Alexander's mission was basically a huge mopping-up operation.

Chapter 3

Alexander Conquers the World (Part II)

With Gaugamela won, Alexander was able to march unopposed into Babylon. At this time Babylon was over 2,000 years old. The city had been a recognized centre of civilization for centuries even before it fell to the Persian armies of Cyrus the Great in 539 BC. The capture of Babylon had transformed the Persians from a warrior people on the fringes of civilization to a recognized world power. Babylon itself had become the Persian administrative capital for Mesopotamia. Therefore, when Alexander took the city he did so as carefully as possible. He wanted no looting, killing, slave-taking or any of the usual indignities suffered by a captured city as this would prevent Babylon from continuing to administer a substantial part of Alexander's new empire.

The treatment of Babylon was the clearest indication yet that Alexander's invasion was not intended simply to destroy the Persian Empire and so make the world safe for Macedon and Greece. By preserving intact the administrative machinery of his new conquests, Alexander showed that he intended also to preserve the Persian Empire itself. Although, naturally, that empire would be under new management. This was not what many in the Hellenistic League had expected. Doubtless many had believed that Alexander's invasion was a huge plundering raid which would end with the Greeks withdrawing to an approximation of their previous frontiers, leaving their homelands safe for generations to come.

Alexander's slow evolution from Macedonian battle-king to quasi-Persian emperor was to cause deep unease and treasonous mutterings in the royal court for the remainder of Alexander's life. More to the point, it was also to cause considerable upset in Alexander's army. Most soldiers had signed up for a campaign of conquest. The prospect of being an army of occupation for the indefinite future filled with alarm men who had ideas of returning home to ancestral lands and family. Yet, after Gaugamela,

Alexander seemed bent on not only taking over the remainder of Darius' empire, but everything beyond that which he could lay hands on.

While it was important to preserve Babylon as an administrative centre for his empire, Alexander had other plans for Susa and Persepolis, the ancient capitals of Persia itself. Alexander needed to demonstrate to the Egyptians and peoples of the Levant that he was not simply replacing Darius as the Persian king – a demonstration which was all the more important as he apparently intended to do just that.

With Susa and Persepolis, the first thing was to secure these two cities before their garrisons were fully up to speed with the fact that Darius' regime had been toppled. Persepolis and Susa were of great political significance, but of more immediate importance was the fact that they were also royal treasuries. Running an empire and maintaining a conquering army were expensive propositions and Alexander wanted that money. The last thing he wanted was rump elements of the previous regime getting their hands on the stored financial power of the Persian Empire and using the money to make his rule more difficult. The second last thing Alexander wanted was for the garrisons of the two cities to realize that the collapse of Darius' rule meant that there was nothing to stop them looting the treasuries for themselves before spontaneously disbanding.

Once Alexander had secured the royal treasuries, he destroyed Persepolis. It is clear from archaeological excavations that Persepolis was not spontaneously burned down by Alexander and his friends after a drunken party, as tradition alleges. Alexander stayed at Persepolis for several months, and during that time the city was systematically looted. Only then was it burned to the ground. It is sometimes claimed (and even Alexander's propaganda promoted the idea) that this was revenge for the burning of Athens by the Persians two hundred years previously. This suggestion was certainly helpful to Alexander's image as a pan-Hellenic leader. However, in propaganda terms it was even more important to make clear to the Egyptians, the Jews and other people who had chafed under Persian rule that the Persian Empire had fallen. The news that the Persian capital had gone up in flames was a powerful affirmation of that fall, and one which obfuscated the fact that Alexander was in reality positioning himself to take over the empire as a going concern.

This intention became even clearer when Alexander set out in pursuit of Darius. Though defeated and driven from the heartland of his empire, Darius was, in theory, still master of extensive domains in Parthia and lands even further east. The problem for Darius was that he had a serious credibility problem. The loyalty of Persian satraps to the king had in the past been ensured by the power of the Persian army. That army had been destroyed at Gaugamela, and in his flight eastwards Darius was more of a supplicant seeking refuge than a commander taking control of the remnants of his empire.

One satrap who might have been presumed to be loyal was Bessus, satrap of Bactria. Bessus was a relative of Darius, and had commanded one wing of his army in the defeat at Gaugamela. Nevertheless, it was Bessus who led the conspiracy which deposed Darius and replaced him with King Artaxerxes V, which was the royal name chosen by Bessus for himself. Bessus probably hoped to placate Alexander by trading the deposed Darius to Alexander in return for recognition of his title as king and perhaps the right to retain the lands of his satrapy. This was not an unrealistic hope (at least one other satrap had already surrendered on favourable terms) had not Bessus taken the title of king – a title which Alexander wanted for himself.

Consequently any offer that Bessus/Artaxerxes made was contemptuously rejected, and the Macedonian armies drove hard to the east with the evident intention of capturing Darius for themselves – and his self-appointed successor along with him. With Alexander closing in fast, Darius became a hindrance rather than the bargaining chip which Bessus had hoped he would be.

The story is that Darius was stabbed and left to die while Bessus sought sanctuary across the River Oxus. The Macedonians came across Darius who, before expiring, managed to gasp out the desire that Alexander should become his heir and successor. If that is how things happened, they could not have turned out better for Alexander. Darius was dead, Alexander his legitimate heir, and Bessus a renegade regicide. It could not have happened more conveniently, which is grounds enough for strong suspicion that it didn't, and that the official story was massaged to a considerable distance from the truth.

Nevertheless, Alexander was now the officially designated ruler of the Persian Empire, which meant that when Bessus was captured he suffered the grisly fate of those who conspired against a Persian king. That fate varied from victim to victim, but was always ingeniously sadistic. According to Plutarch, the fate of Bessus was to be slowly torn apart by being tied to young trees bent together for the occasion and then gradually released.

Having ordered the death of Bessus as a Persian king would do, Alexander attempted to live as a Persian king might do. He began to dress in the Persian style and introduced Persian customs at his court. He also ordered that his subjects should prostrate themselves on the ground when they approached him. The performance of this gesture, the *proskynesis*, may have reassured Alexander's Persian subjects of the continuity of their empire. However, it also outraged Alexander's Macedonians who were already deeply suspicious that, instead of destroying the Persian Empire as intended, they had merely swapped that empire's kings.

Cleitus, the man who had saved the life of Alexander during the battle at the Granicus, did not hold back with his accusations that Alexander had betrayed Macedon and his country's traditional ways. That the accusation came in a drunken after-dinner contretemps shows that Alexander had not abandoned at least one disreputable Macedonian habit. Turfed from the royal tent, Cleitus stormed back in to deliver a final retort. Thereupon Alexander seized a javelin, hurled it at Cleitus and killed him on the spot.

Alexander realized that he had gone too far and abandoned the practice of the *proskynesis*. Nevertheless, he held a grudge against those who had opposed him in the matter. These men were accused of treason and executed. Among the dead was the son of Alexander's general, Parmenio. Alexander was too much of a Macedonian to believe for a moment that Parmenio would forgive this act. Therefore, the man who had served Alexander loyally for so long was killed before he was even aware that something was amiss.

Having put his house in order after the turmoil which he was mainly responsible for causing, in 326 BC Alexander turned to the southeast. Bactria was restless, and beyond that the people of Sogdiana were downright mutinous – for all that Alexander had married a Sogdian princess, Roxana, in an attempt to pacify the region. Nevertheless, Alexander wanted to press on and add India to his already sprawling empire.

For the purposes of this narrative there is little need to describe in detail Alexander's Indian campaign. The expedition did not ultimately add to the Hellenistic kingdoms which were created by Alexander's conquests and indeed produced little result other than demonstrating to Alexander that there were indeed worlds left to conquer – and that he was not going to conquer them. The Macedonian expansion had pushed the frontiers of the Greek world to the foothills of the Himalayas, but that expansion stopped at the Ganges.

Alexander massively underestimated the size and resources of the Indian sub-continent. Compared to India the lands of the eastern Persian Empire were underpopulated and poor. Alexander's veteran army, with its unfamiliar weapons and tactics, certainly came as a shock to the Indian kings of the Ganges region, and Alexander won several battles. Nevertheless, unlike Issus and Gaugamela, these victories did not result in wholesale conquest. Instead the Indian kings conceded the battlefield, and mustered the resources to fight Alexander again, and again after that.

Alexander's frustration showed at Massaga, where he was wounded in the ankle while assaulting that stronghold. After he had captured the place Alexander ordered the entire population to be slaughtered.

Alexander's principal opponent in India was a ruler whom the Greeks called Porus (properly Raja Purushottama) who ruled a kingdom called Bharat in the Punjab region of modern Pakistan. Alexander's army won an epic victory at the Battle of the River Hydaspes in May of 326 BC. Porus was defeated and surrendered on very favourable terms, but the aftermath of the battle broke Alexander's army. More precisely, what broke Alexander's army was the realization that while it had taken a tremendous effort to defeat Porus, Porus was not the greatest power in India, or even in the region. Other, mightier states were waiting beyond the Ganges, and others beyond that.

There was simply too much India for the Macedonians to even begin conquering the place, and, unlike their commander, the soldiery were sensible enough to grasp that fact. They mutinied. Very politely, but they mutinied nevertheless. Alexander was informed in no uncertain terms that he was welcome to go on and subdue the sub-continent, but his army was not coming with him. They wanted to go home.

> Do not now lead us on against our will. You will no longer find us the same men in the face of danger, since we face it unwillingly. If it please you, let us return to our homeland. You can see your mother, organize the affairs of the Greeks and celebrate in the home of your fathers those many and great victories which you have won. Then by all means, let us launch another expedition, maybe against these very Indians to the east, or if you prefer north to the Euxine [Black Sea], or the furthermost reaches beyond Libya.
>
> (Speech of Coenus to Alexander in Arrian 5.27)

Alexander had no choice. He was forced to make what arrangements he could and then withdrew. He left such volunteers as he could in garrisons which backed up the rule of Porus and Taxiles; conquered kings-turned-satrap who were to administer Alexander's Indian conquests. The more fortunate part of Alexander's army was sent east to occupy the former Persian domains of southern Iran. The unfortunate part of the army was led by Alexander himself in a march along the shores of the Arabian Sea on the way back to Susa and the heartlands of the empire.

These shores were part of the infamous Gedrosian Desert, a desert which the founder of the Persian Empire, Cyrus the Great, had failed to cross. Alexander was a great admirer of Cyrus. He had executed men who – presumably in an attempt to curry his favour – had desecrated Cyrus' tomb, and now it seemed that he wanted to make the point that he could succeed where Cyrus had not. Naturally, this would cause considerable suffering to the army, but it was quite possible that in Alexander's present state of mind, suffering was precisely what he intended.

In any case, it was a spectacularly bone-headed and pointless manoeuvre which cost the lives of an estimated 12,000 of Alexander's men, and the uncounted deaths of countless servants and other camp followers. The main thing that the 60-day march achieved was to put Alexander out of touch with his new empire for two months, during which time there was considerable uncertainty whether he was alive or not.

As on a previous occasion when the king had been severely ill, things ground to a halt without his guiding hand. A number of satraps had used Alexander's absence to develop a dangerous degree of autonomy, and others had been quietly amassing what amounted to private armies in readiness for the anarchy which would inevitably break loose if Alexander failed to emerge alive from the desert.

Emerge alive Alexander did, and in no very good temper. He had shared the privations of his army while on the march, enduring heat, hunger and lack of water alongside his men. Like his men he was looking for someone – other than himself – to take the blame for the debacle. The charge that incompetent or treacherous subordinates had failed to send supplies (supplies that they may not have known they were supposed to provide) allowed Alexander both to execute some of his more independent-minded satraps and also mollify the army to some degree.

There were rumblings from further afield, back home in Macedon. Alexander had left his homeland under the steady hand of Antipater, one of Philip II's old commanders. The veteran general had much to cope with, starting with the rampaging Persian navy which caused unrest up and down the Aegean until Alexander's victory at Issus cut the supply line of the fleet. Once Alexander had also deprived the Persians of their Phoenician supply bases the hostile fleet dispersed, moving a lively rebellion in Thrace to the top of Antipater's list of problems.

As he was subduing the rebellious Thracians, word reached Antipater that the Spartans had taken advantage of his preoccupations in the north and inspired the Arcadians to rebel against Macedon. (Because they had never joined the Hellenic League, the Spartans were not rebelling against Macedon, but their actions certainly constituted an act of war.)

Faced with two emergencies, Antipater chose to deal with the most urgent – the rebellion in Greece. The leader of the Thracian rebellion – a Macedonian governor called Memnon – was surprised and gratified to discover that he would be allowed to surrender and even keep his job provided that he paid a large fine and supplied men to Antipater's Greek campaign.

The Greek campaign was hard work. The Spartans fought with their customary stubbornness but Antipater had troops every bit as well-trained and experienced and he had many more of them. The two armies clashed near the city of Megalopolis in Arcadia in 331 BC, and the Spartans were defeated and their king slain.

While Antipater was all in favour of doing to Sparta as Alexander had done to Thebes, Alexander himself, flush with his victories over Darius, was inclined to be magnanimous. By way of belittling Antipater's victory he remarked to his courtiers: 'It appears that there has been a battle of mice in Arcadia'. He then ordered the Spartans to pay a modest fine and compelled their entry into the Hellenic League.

One reason for Alexander's apparent jealousy of Antipater's achievements was because Alexander's mother Olympias had been sending a non-stop stream of accusations and invective against Antipater almost from the time that Alexander had left for Asia. Olympias had a highly unstable character, and bitterly resented Antipater for keeping her excesses in check.

One of Alexander's more unpleasant tasks after emerging from the desert was to wade through a two-month backlog of such letters. Deciding that tensions between his mother and the Macedonian regent had reached a dangerous level, Alexander ordered Antipater to join him in Asia with a fresh levy of troops. A veteran general of Alexander's was returning to Macedon with discharged veterans, and this man would take up the delicate job of handling the Hellenic League and Olympias.

The suspicious Antipater dithered. He was well aware that a summons to the royal court could be a precursor to summary charges and execution, so he took as much time as he could in gathering the required soldiers – a delay that ultimately paid off.

In fact, Antipater could legitimately claim that good men were hard to find, for Alexander's conquests had drained both Macedon and Greece of manpower. This was partly because almost an entire generation of young recruits had marched off to the East and not returned. While a handful of veterans were discharged back to Macedon, Alexander had a habit of founding cities along the route of his conquests. By now there were over a dozen new cities called Alexandria alone, apart from at least that number of foundations with alternative names. These included Bucephela, named after Alexander's favourite horse which had died in India.

All of these cities were populated with startled locals who had been rounded up from nearby villages and combined with Macedonian veterans discharged or injured after recent fighting. This tendency to found cities wherever possible was followed by Alexander's successors, and the effect was to seed Asia Minor and points east with centres of Hellenic culture which were to endure for the next millennium.

However, the spread of the Greek world from Ephesus to Kandahar (Kandahar was founded by Alexander in 330 BC and is today the second-largest city in Afghanistan) meant that the Greeks were spread relatively thin in Greece itself. Greece was always better at producing philosophers than grain. Eighty per cent of the country is mountainous and crops grow poorly in much of the remainder. Given the chance to move east to the fertile plains of Lydia, Mesopotamia or the Nile Delta, many Greek peasants leapt at the chance. Artisans and merchants also scented opportunity in the new cities being strewn across the Asian hinterland and left the Greek mainland to seek their fortunes.

Even more than the constant inter-city wars which had plagued the Greek peninsula from the fifth century onwards, and even more than the devastation later caused by Roman armies, it was the massive depopulation caused by the lure of the Hellenic settlements to the east which meant that Greece was little more than a quiet backwater for the remainder of antiquity.

The influx of new arrivals in his cities and his armies presented Alexander with something of a quandary. While immigration had added a Greek tinge to his empire, the majority of the population were native peoples accustomed to Persian rule. Therefore, if he was not to spend his time battling continuous rebellions (and the prolonged rebellion in Sogdiana in the east had destroyed any taste he might have had for this), Alexander had to find a way to make himself acceptable to his new subjects.

The obvious way to do this was to take up where Darius had left off, and run the Persian Empire as a Persian king – all the while protesting to the Egyptians and restive peoples of the Levant that things were now completely different. The problem with this approach was that a Macedonian war-leader and a Persian king were completely different roles. While the Persians were mollified and reassured by Alexander's adoption of Persian dress and customs, the Macedonians and other Greek were startled and horrified to the same degree. And while the Greeks in Asia were very few, they were also very influential.

The most influential of all were Alexander's own soldiers. In resisting Alexander's plans to conquer the Indian sub-continent the army had already forced Alexander to back down once. Now the men threatened to mutiny again if Alexander did not demote Persians he had promoted to high office, and demobilize those Persian military units he had raised. Alexander was aware of what was at stake. Instead of concessions he raised the stakes. Those Persians in high command were promoted further, and the titles of some Macedonian units were transferred to their Persian counterparts. One Macedonian-style Persian unit (possibly of the children of mixed Persian-Greek unions) was named 'the Successors' – as clear a threat as Alexander could make to his mutinous men.

This time it was the army which backed down. The men pleaded with Alexander to forgive them. Alexander did so, but pushed his point further home in a marriage ceremony in the Persian city of Susa. Here Alexander added another wife to his collection. This time the blushing bride was Barsine Stateira, the eldest daughter of the late King Darius. Since tradition allowed both Persian and Macedonian kings multiple wives this marriage met with few objections (history does not record how Barsine felt about it) and strengthened Alexander's claim to the Persian throne.

Nor did Alexander marry alone. Overall, some eighty of his top-ranking officers were married to daughters of the Persian nobility on the same occasion. All the marriages were conducted in the Persian style. The message was clear. Alexander intended not a Hellenistic empire in the East but a Persian-Greek fusion which would combine the strongest elements of each culture.

This was a highly advanced concept, and one which, had Alexander's successors followed through, might well have produced a truly enduring and remarkable civilization. It is also an extraordinarily sophisticated concept for a warrior king whose previous method of dealing with resistance had involved terror and wholesale massacre. Therefore it is reasonable to ask what outside influences might have influenced Alexander's approach.

The obvious candidate is Aristotle of Stageira. Aristotle (384–322 BC) was the outstanding philosopher of his day and had been Alexander's tutor since 343 BC. Tutor and student were close and Alexander often sent rare plant and animal specimens home for Aristotle to examine. Yet, for all his generally liberal approach to politics and ethics, Aristotle – whose name means 'with the best intentions' – was an unashamed Greek chauvinist. As far as he was concerned, the living species consisted of Greeks, other humans and beasts, and very much in that order. Far from encouraging Alexander's Perseophilia, Aristotle was appalled by it. He so strongly urged Alexander to change course that the disagreement led to an estrangement between the two which was never reconciled.

Therefore we have to look elsewhere to find the origins of Alexander's very untypical behaviour. Alexander's mother Olympias we can dismiss out of hand, since Olympias' preferred solution to any problem was to kill the people causing it, and to do so as sadistically as possible. (Which was one reason for her poor relationship with the calmly rational Antipater.)

A good argument can be made that the idea for a Persian-Greek fusion came originally from Alexander's father, Philip II. Philip was no idealist, but while integrating Greek and Persian cultures is a noble concept, it also would have worked well at the level of practical politics. We see something of the same attitude in Philip's approach to Greece, where he quickly changed the perception of a Macedonian conquest into Macedonian leadership of a pan-Hellenic alliance. Philip did not make subjects of former enemies, he made them into allies. How much Alexander adopted his father's plans for a post-conquest Persian Empire will never be known, so at this point we shall note that Alexander's approach to his new subjects was novel, out of character, and not adopted by his successors, and leave aside further speculation about this anomaly.

In 324 BC Alexander suffered a deep personal blow. His childhood companion and present right-hand man, Hephaestion, died and in so doing deprived Alexander of a loyal and competent supporter. In later eras there has been considerable speculation that Alexander and Hephaestion were lovers, a viewpoint which tends to downgrade Hephaestion to the status of concubine while overlooking his considerable skills as a diplomat, scholar and soldier. Hephaestion was both a boyhood friend and Alexander's present most-trusted confidant and advisor – it seems superfluous to make him a lover as well, especially given that the evidence for this is decidedly scanty. Homosexual relationships between adult Greek males was unusual, and even more so among Macedonians who tended towards the more macho forms of Greek culture. While sexual relationship is certainly possible, we need not accept its existence to believe that Alexander was devastated by the loss of a companion whom he had once called 'the second part of Alexander'.

Hephaestion was also the main supporter of Alexander's pro-Persian policy. In the weddings at Susa, Hephaestion had married another of Darius' daughters. Thus his death was not only a severe blow to Alexander at the personal level, it also meant that he had lost a close ally whose skill at personal relationships had kept the warring factions in the royal court off each others' throats.

It is a mystery why Hephaestion, a young man in the prime of life, should have suddenly died after seven days of illness – especially as he seemed to be recuperating right at the end. This has led to speculation that he was poisoned by one of his many enemies at court. This is certainly possible, though it should be noted that Macedonian political killers usually preferred a direct approach featuring sharp-edged instruments. It is also notable that Hephaestion ignored his doctor's advice and ate a large meal washed down with abundant wine just before he died. This would have certainly not have helped a perforated ulcer or burst appendix.

Hephaestion was given a lavish funeral in Babylon, and 'lavish' here means probably a more expensive send-off than heretofore given to any human on the planet. According to Plutarch the entire funeral was costed at 10,000 talents. While translation into modern values is difficult, by a rough estimate this would allow the entire population of Athens to live comfortably for a year, or one skilled artisan and his family to take the next three-quarters of a million years off work.

Alexander's plans for yet further monuments and memorials for his companion were interrupted by his own sudden illness. Exactly what caused this is uncertain. There is disagreement among our different sources (Arrian, Cassius Dio, Plutarch), but all are unanimous that Alexander had been drinking heavily beforehand.

What exactly ailed Alexander during his twelve days illness has been a matter of considerable debate ever since. A contemporary report of his symptoms is reasonably detailed.

Plate 1: Busts of Alexander the Great were common in the ancient world, where he was seen as an inspirational figure. (*Public domain picture*)

Plate 2: I Demetrios the First of Bactria, wearing his elephant head-dress. Detail from a contemporary coin. (*P. Matyszak*)

Plate 3: Bronze bust of Seleucus I Nicator. (*Massimo Finizio via Wikimedia Creative Commons*)

Plate 4: It is uncertain which Ptolemaic queen is depicted in this bust but reasonably certain her name was Cleopatra, Arsinoe or Bernice. (*Metropolitan Museum of Art, New York*)

Plate 8: Detail of a carving of a Hellenistic cavalryman, highlighting the linothorax linen cuirass. Though depicted bareback, cavalry such as this used saddles, albeit without stirrups. (*P. Matyszak*)

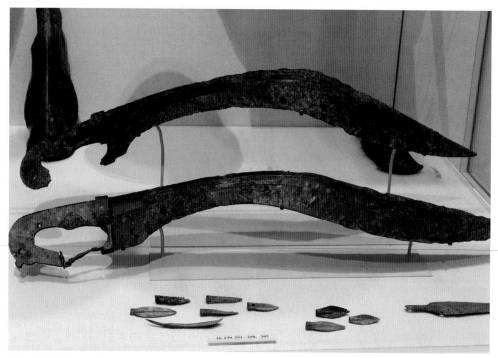

Plate 9: Kopis-style swords were slashing weapons designed for use when the hoplite formation had broken down. (*Metropolitan Museum of Art, New York; Picture copyright of P. Matyszak*)

Plate 10: The charge of the Persian chariots at Gaugamela, as imagined by French artist Andre Castaigne 1861–1929.

Plate 11: Funerary slab for a Hellenistic soldier. While the painting is damaged, the soldier can still be seen taking a cup from his attendant. (*Metropolitan Museum of Art, New York*)

Plate 12: The Agora of Smyrna, built during the Hellenistic era at the base of Pagos Hill, Izmir, Turkey. Wholesale urbanism was a feature of the early Hellenistic period. (*Picture: Carole Raddato via Wikimedia, Creative Commons*)

Plate 13: Print of the Great Altar at Pergamon as reconstructed from the archaeological remains. (*Friedrich Thierch 1882*)

Plate 14: The market gate of Miletus, once on the Ionian coast of Anatolia, now reassembled in the Pergamon Museum in Berlin. (*Picture: public domain*)

Plate 15: Elephant on the obverse of a coin of Antiochus III of Seleucia. The legend reads 'King Antiochus'. (*Picture: public domain*)

Plate 16: The theatre at Syracuse. Hellenistic culture was widespread, and classic plays by writers such as Euripides were shared by audiences from Iberia to Mesopotamia. (*Ewa Shah*)

The *Pharos* of PTOLOMEY King of Egypt

Plate 17: A print from an early modern encyclopaedia showing a reconstruction of what the Lighthouse at Alexandria may have looked like.

Plate 18: Section of a cuneiform tablet from Mesopotamia. Despite the Greek presence, native languages were often used for administration. (*Public domain*)

He partied and drank at the house of Medius, and after rising from there he took a bath and again drank late into the night. After that he ate a little and slept on the premises, as he was already feeling a touch feverish. ...

[Two days later] The fever had now consumed him all night without remission. The next day he bathed and offered sacrifices ... notwithstanding that he now had a dangerously high fever he summoned his officers and gave them their instructions. ...

Another day went by. Although gravely ill Alexander refused to neglect religious observances. ... Then he was removed from the park [where he had been staying] back to the royal palace. Though he seemed aware of his officers when he saw them, he could no longer speak. ... He struggled to raise his head as each man went by, and it was clear from his eyes that he recognized them.

[some of Alexander's generals] asked the God Serapis if it would be better for Alexander to be carried into his temple, but the god refused this, and said it would be better for Alexander to stay where he was. ... soon afterwards Alexander died.

(*The Palace diaries* as quoted in Arrian
7.26 and Plutarch, *Alexander*, 76)

At the time of his death Alexander was thirty-two years old. This, even by the lower standards of the ancient world was generally considered to be close to the prime of life. Suspicion as to what killed Alexander immediately turned to the question of poison. Disease is another possibility. Typhoid fever has been suggested, though there was no recorded outbreak either before or after Alexander's death. Malaria might also be the cause, but the ancients were familiar with the disease and Alexander's reported symptoms do not match well with malaria anyway.

An intriguing possibility is that he consumed a native local plant called Veratum, which is deadly if fermented. This might have been deliberately or accidentally (the plant closely resembles garlic) administered to Alexander at the house of Medius. However, poisoning an ancient ruler was tricky because kings tended to share their wine and platters with everyone at the table. This helped everyone to feel valued and included, but it also meant that everyone at the table would be included among the victims if poison was slipped into the food.

It is said that as Alexander was expiring, someone asked if the worst should happen and Alexander died of illness, then who was to inherit his empire? Alexander replied 'The strongest' (or 'the most capable'). In other words, the field was open.

That Alexander should not have specified an heir might be considered unusual given that his high-risk lifestyle meant he could die at any time. Yet he did not name an heir precisely because he did not wish his life to become even more risky. The trouble with heirs is that they are well aware that the king making them so might change his mind, and if a different person becomes king things are unlikely to end well for the former heir, who by definition also once had a good claim to the throne. Furthermore, once an heir is nominated a faction forms about him, consisting of those who hope to benefit once the old regime passes away.

In other words once an heir is nominated, it becomes in his interest and in the interest of his supporters that he should inherit as speedily as possible. After all, once a king was dead it became extremely unhealthy to enquire what part the successor played in arranging that death. So Alexander left the question open of who was to inherit his empire. It is to that empire that we now turn.

The most significant thing about Alexander's empire is that it was huge – a landmass that was far greater than that of the later Roman Empire. It stretched from the shores of the Adriatic Sea in the west all the way to the foothills of the Himalayas in the east. If the empire of Alexander had existed today it would be one of the largest countries in the world by area. A flight from Athens to Kandahar takes eight hours, and all of it is over lands conquered by Alexander.

Not only was the new Macedonian Empire large, it was also enormously diverse. Some of Alexander's subjects were herdsmen and nomads whose lives had barely changed since the Stone Age. These peoples were barely aware that anyone ruled them at all, let alone that their new king came from a place they had never heard of. On the other hand, there were those places largely responsible for dragging the rest of mankind out of the Stone Age – civilizations such as those of Mesopotamia and Egypt, not to mention the heirs of now-extinct cultures such as the Luwains, and Hittites in Asia Minor, and the peoples of the Levant. (Even now Damascus in Syria can fairly claim to be the oldest continuously inhabited place on Earth.)

Phoenicians, Egyptians, Hebrews, Greeks, Persians, Indians – all these peoples had their own ancient and diverse political structures, economic systems and social hierarchies which had to be united under a single leader. The Persians had almost made it work, but even their empire was not as diverse at that of Alexander. Later generations were in awe of Alexander and his conquests. Yet Alexander died before he could seriously begin the far greater challenge – that of ruling what he had taken. That was a task that now fell to Alexander's successor – whoever that turned out to be.

Chapter 4

The Wars of the Diadochi ('Successors')

Being a high-ranking Macedonian commander was a risky business. As Alexander and Hephaestion had recently demonstrated, illness could take a man from healthy to a corpse in a matter of days. Also, as Macedonian commanders were expected to lead from the front, death in battle offered even swifter passage to the Underworld. Finally, life in a Macedonian court was itself risky – and short too, if the king rightly or wrongly suspected that a subordinate had become treasonous.

Although the Macedonians had no designated successor to Alexander, there were a number of men with the rank and training to step into Alexander's shoes if need be. The exigencies of the job meant that these were hard, ruthless men, accustomed to death and possessing hardly a scruple between the lot of them. Because each of them was qualified for Alexander's job, this meant that every one of the group represented a threat to each of the others. The struggle for power after Alexander's death is the story of how these rivals engaged in realpolitik, shifting alliances, back-stabbing and betrayal on a truly epic scale. It is time to meet the protagonists.

Perdiccas, Commander of the Cavalry

The Companion Cavalry were the elite unit in the Macedonian army, and the commander had the prestige and authority that went with the rank. Perdiccas was from the Macedonian nobility, and had supported Alexander from the beginning. He had been badly wounded when suppressing the Theban revolt of 335 BC, but had recovered to fight alongside Alexander throughout the Persian campaign. He had dutifully married the daughter of a Persian aristocrat during Alexander's mass wedding at Susa, but put the unfortunate bride aside on Alexander's death. In terms of rank, nobility and prestige, Perdiccas was considered the leading candidate to take Alexander's place.

Antipater, Viceroy of Macedon

The calm, steady Antipater was at this time one of the most unpopular men in the entire Greek world. Ruling Macedon in Alexander's name meant also controlling the Hellenic League, aggressive barbarians, the rebellious Thracians, the bellicose Spartans and Alexander's mother, the insufferable Olympias. (The latter task was made easier in that Olympias had temporarily returned to her native land of Epirus to serve as regent for her young cousin.)

The Hellenic League disliked Antipater because it was Antipater who had to enforce Alexander's insatiable need for grain and manpower. The Spartans loathed Antipater because he had broken them in battle and forced them into an unwelcome alliance. Olympias found Antipater an unwelcome check on her irrational and sadistic impulsiveness, and had finally prevailed on Alexander to have him replaced. Antipater was in his seventies at this point, and age had made him wise enough to prevaricate long enough until the situation changed radically on Alexander's death.

With a desperately unstable Greek peninsula and an even more unstable Olympias to deal with, Antipater had enough on his plate at home without getting involved with affairs in the rest of the empire. Nor did anyone particularly want Antipater's job, apart from an ambitious son called Cassander, who indeed was eager to take over his father's mantle.

Antigonus Monophthalmus, Satrap of Greater Phrygia

Another of Alexander's long-term supporters, Antigonus had originally served with Philip II before giving his support to the young Alexander. He had been with Alexander through the entire Persian conquest. In the Issus campaign he had operated independently and competently in defeating a Persian counterattack and an attempt by Greek mercenaries to sever the Macedonian lines of communication. Like Antipater, Antigonus was in his late seventies, though of undiminished ambition and vigour. He too had a son, a young man called Demetrios. Father and son were on excellent terms. This was a rarity among the Macedonian aristocracy, and the fact that each could trust the other would prove to be a huge asset.

Ptolemy, Junior General

Despite his relatively low rank, Ptolemy was of aristocratic birth on his mother's side. Rumour suggested that he was an illegitimate son of Philip II, though this may have been a later fabrication. Certainly Alexander did not hold Ptolemy's birth against him, and the two were friends from boyhood onwards. Alexander trusted Ptolemy completely, and as one of the king's ceremonial bodyguards, Ptolemy was one of the few armed men allowed into the royal presence.

No-one expected the relatively low-ranking Ptolemy to strive for mastery of Alexander's empire. He was a quiet man who had fought well at the Battle of Issus, and had played a leading part in the campaign to capture Bessus, the regicidal would-be successor to the defeated King Darius. Ptolemy had seen much of the world as a general of Alexander, but evidently the part that had impressed him most was Egypt. Ptolemy had accompanied Alexander on his travels through that ancient land and was clearly taken with its potential. Egypt was currently ruled by a satrap appointed by Alexander, but Ptolemy began to lobby for command of the place for himself.

Eumenes, the Outsider

Loyal, scholarly and highly competent, Eumenes had served Philip II with distinction. On Philip's assassination, he supported Alexander, and was rewarded with a series of administrative posts. No-one doubted Eumenes' loyalty to Alexander and his family, but despite this the man was generally despised. This was because Eumenes came from Cardia in Thrace and was suspected of having Scythian origins.

This did not greatly bother either Philip or Alexander, as the pair were remarkably open-minded on that count, but it certainly bothered the soldiers who did not like to be commanded by a 'foreigner'. It is somewhat ironic that the Macedonians, who had for generations resented the southern Greeks for considering them 'barbarians', now did the same thing to an otherwise exemplary general.

Seleucus, the Underdog

The origins of Seleucus are uncertain. It is probable his mother was called Laodice, since this became a family name in later generations (rather as female Ptolemies tended to be called Cleopatra). The family was certainly noble, as Seleucus served as a page to Philip II, a position open only to sons of the nobility.

While in his twenties, Seleucus joined Alexander in the invasion of Persia. His ability at command saw him promoted to leadership of the 'Silver Shields', the elite Macedonian infantry unit. He served with distinction in the east and in India, and while in Sogdiana he picked up a princess called Apama. Seleucus made his relationship official when he married the woman in the mass wedding at Susa. Unlike most other marriages on that occasion this one endured, and Apama gave Seleucus at least two children, a son named Antiochus and a daughter named (inevitably) Laodice.

This gang of six made up the leading characters in the unsavoury drama which now unfolded. While most of the above had a chance of ruling Alexander's empire, the actual status of king was not immediately available. There were many in the army who wanted to remain loyal to the line of Alexander, so any ruler would (for now) have to be content with the title of regent. There was a candidate for king right there in the camp – Arrhidaeus, a son of Philip II by another of his many wives. Arrhidaeus suffered from a mental disability of uncertain severity – the result, claims Plutarch, of an unsuccessful poisoning attempt by Olympias when the lad was a youngster. While many modern historians are sceptical of this claim, it is reasonably certain that Alexander took his half-brother along with him to prevent Olympias from doing him any further harm.

Just to complicate things further, Alexander's bride, Roxana, was pregnant and due to give birth. If she produced a son (and she did) then this child of Alexander would have massive appeal to the troops. Among Alexander's commanders a furious debate developed as to what course of action to follow. In the end Perdiccas prevailed with a compromise solution. Arrhidaeus should be promoted to king and take the name of Philip III of Macedon – king, but not the ruler. That job would be held by Perdiccas himself who would act as regent for Alexander's posthumous son, who was also called Alexander.

The First Division ('The Partition of Babylon')

The remaining generals were each pacified with satrapies in different parts of Alexander's empire; satrapies which each began busily to convert into a personal fiefdom and power base. (Apart from Seleucus who was not considered powerful enough to merit his own satrapy. Instead Seleucus got Perdiccas' old job as commander of the cavalry.) This division of the empire is sometimes called 'The Partition of Babylon'.

As his generals dispersed to their new domains, Perdiccas had to deal with a daughter of Philip II who had hurried to Babylon on the news of Alexander's death. This daughter planned to marry her own daughter, a strong-willed lass called Eurydice, to the new King Philip III. In character, Arrhidaeus/Philip was a highly-amenable fellow whom Perdiccas had little trouble controlling. Arrhidaeus as a potential glove puppet manipulated by the formidable Eurydice was a different proposition, and Perdiccas took violent steps to prevent the union.

Eurydice managed to escape assassination, though her mother did not, and the indignation of the troops at the killing forced Perdiccas to allow the marriage to Arrhidaeus. This killing, and the assiduous spadework of Eurydice thereafter, combined to undermine Perdiccas' standing with the army and the regent was never fully secure thereafter.

Alexander's death had caused shock waves through the empire, and its new overlords were initially busy suppressing a series of rebellions. Antipater probably had the hardest job, as the Athenians led a coalition of Greek cities in an uprising which for a while had Antipater penned into a fortress at Lamia. (From whence the rebellion gets its name of the Lamian War of 323–322 BC). Antipater was saved by the arrival of those discharged veteran troops whom Alexander had sent home (p.47) and he made peace by picking off each city in the Athenian alliance with the offer of favourable terms.

Eumenes moved to Anatolia and with his usual quiet competence suppressed unrest in the region. There was also trouble in the far east, in Bactria. The many Greeks whom Alexander had settled in the region made a determined effort to return home, and had to be turned back by armed force.

Ptolemy had been behind the scenes furiously negotiating the virtual partition of Alexander's empire between his most powerful generals. He wanted, and got, command of Egypt which he was to rule as a sort of satrap of Perdiccas (the actual arrangement was considerably more complex). Egypt was at the time being run by an appointee of Alexander called Cleomenes who had immediately taken advantage of Alexander's death to extend his power. Ptolemy did not immediately displace Cleomenes, but instead put a stop to the man's depredations (Cleomenes had something of a talent for extortion) and placed Cleomenes under his direct command.

There matters rested uneasily until the delicate balance was upset by Olympias. Annoyed by the coup of Eurydice in marrying Arrhidaeus, Olympias decided to move her family back to the centre of power by offering her daughter – Alexander's sister – as a bride to Perdiccas.

This upset the applecart because firstly, Perdiccas was already due to marry Antipater's daughter in a dynastic alliance. Antipater took the breaking of the engagement as a personal betrayal. Secondly, both the current royals were of disputable legitimacy – Arrhidaeus because of his mental handicap, and Alexander junior because of his half-Oriental origins. Should Perdiccas and Alexander's full sister (another Cleopatra) produce a boy child between them, then the army would enthusiastically endorse the boy as king. This would allow Perdiccas as the boy's father to leverage his temporary position as regent into a permanent job.

There were other strains in the alliance. In Anatolia the kingdom of Cappadocia remained outside the empire, bypassed by Alexander in his rush to the Levant and the East. Perdiccas set out to conquer the place, and ordered Antigonus – the nearest successor general – to supply the men and the money. Antigonus saw no reason why he should fund the march to glory of a rival, and simply ignored the order. When Perdiccas demanded that Antigonus appear at his court and explain himself, Antigonus allied himself with Antipater instead.

Things got worse for the embattled regent. Alexander's remains (probably preserved in honey, as was the custom) were on the way to Macedonia where a magnificent tomb had been prepared to receive him. But the body never got there. While the funeral train was moving through Syria it was hijacked by minions of Ptolemy, who blandly informed the world of Alexander's (hitherto undisclosed) wish to be buried in Alexandria.

This was more than a propaganda move. A Macedonian king was buried by his successor, so in taking possession of Alexander's corpse and seeing to its interment, Ptolemy was assuming the role of a king. Just to rub in his point, Ptolemy invaded and took possession of Cyrenaica, a region outside his original sphere of command. When Perdiccas furiously revoked Ptolemy's command and ordered him to hand control of Egypt back to Cleomenes, Ptolemy executed the man instead. This was outright mutiny, and Perdiccas had no choice but to act. He declared Ptolemy a rebel and moved his army south. In response, Antipater and Antigonus promptly declared their support for Ptolemy.

Eumenes, loyal as ever, stuck with the current regime and inflicted a nasty setback on the northern rebel alliance in a battle in Cappadocia. His efforts were for naught, because Perdiccas was far less successful in the south. One of the things that had attracted Ptolemy to Egypt was that the country was eminently defensible. He had the Red Sea on one side of the country and the Mediterranean in the north. The sea of sand to the west made an impenetrable barrier, so the only access to the country for an invader was by way of Gaza. Thousands of years of repelling invaders who had taken that route meant that the Egyptians had built some formidable defences in Gaza. Perdiccas was no Alexander, and his attack quickly stalled.

This was the last straw for the army who had never been too keen on Perdiccas in the first place. To the general relief of the men, Perdiccas was assassinated and the attack on Egypt was called off. The leader of the assassins was the commander of the cavalry, Seleucus. Seleucus now took command of the army, and proposed to his fellow successor generals that the partition of the empire needed renegotiating.

The Rise of Cassander

A complex realignment took place, with the main changes being as follows. Antipater was made the overall leader of the empire. This was probably because he had troubles enough in Macedon and Greece and was unlikely to interfere with the domains of others as aggressively as

Perdiccas had done. Seleucus was rewarded for his deft knife-work with command of Babylonia. The joint kings, Alexander and Arrhidaeus, were to be moved to Macedon where Antipater could keep an eye on them. All well and good, but hardly had the new terms been agreed when everything was again upset in 319 BC with the inconsiderate death of Antipater.

Just to make things worse, Antipater had named as his successor not his (overly) ambitious son, Cassander, but the relatively unknown Polyperchon. There was no way that Cassander would accept this. War became inevitable, and just as inevitably, the other Diadochi were drawn into the conflict.

Eumenes, as ever, supported the status quo. For Eumenes, if Antipater had appointed Polyperchon as his successor, then Polyperchon got Eumenes' support. This promptly got Antigonus on Cassander's side – not because Antigonus had anything against Polyperchon but because, after the beating he had been given in the previous round of conflict, Antigonus had unfinished business with Eumenes. Anyway, his conflict with Eumenes had never been officially concluded. Ptolemy joined in on the side of Antigonus mainly because of their former alliance.

However, Ptolemy had no intention of getting involved in actual fighting. The army had offered him Perdiccas' regency after the post had abruptly become vacant, but Ptolemy wisely declined. His ambitions stopped at Egypt. Nevertheless, he watched the fighting with interest and looked for a chance to reclaim those parts of the Levant which had once been part of the domain of the Pharaohs.

Among those doing the actual fighting, the fortunes of war changed and changed again in this, the Second Successor War of 319–315 BC. Cassander drove Polyperchon from Macedonia. The displaced ruler took with him the young king Alexander, while Eurydice and Arrhidaeus sided with Cassander. Olympias held a grudge against Eurydice because she had married Arrhidaeus while her daughter Cleopatra was still unattached after the untimely demise of Perdiccas. Olympias came down on the side of the exiled Polyperchon, and the pair came storming back into Macedon. The army of Arrhidaeus made its feeling plain when they deserted their king and moved wholesale on to the side of Alexander's mother.

This left the royal couple of Arrhidaeus and Eurydice at the mercy of Olympias. Arrhidaeus was too dangerous for anything but immediate execution, but Polyperchon wanted to hold on to Eurydice as a bargaining chip in a dynastic wedding deal. Even this proved dangerous, as the army started to show signs of dangerous sympathy for the imprisoned queen. Helpful as ever, Olympias sent Eurydice a rope, a dagger and a cup of hemlock and told her to choose. Eurydice took the rope and hanged herself.

Cassander had not been present at the desertion of Arrhidaeus' army. He had his own men, and these stayed loyal. Olympias proved better at killing than fighting, and was anyway hampered by the low morale of her own men. These were discomfited at the wholesale massacre of fellow-countrymen suspected of being supporters of Cassander; for Olympias did not stop with killing only Arrhidaeus and Eurydice. Olympias ended up besieged with the remnants of her army at Pydna (near the site of a later famous battle with the Romans in 168 BC). Despite the best efforts of Polyperchon to get a relief force to her, Olympias was finally forced to surrender. She did this because Cassander had promised to spare her life. He lied.

Olympias was executed in 316 BC. Many modern writers feel that Olympias was given rough treatment by ancient historians who considered her too aggressive and politically active for a 'proper' woman. This is undoubtedly true; however, it does feminism an injustice to maintain that women can be just as hard and ruthless as males. The very aspects of her personality that led her to defy the stereotyped gender roles of her day were probably also those that led her to disregard many of the prevailing ethical considerations as well.

Polyperchon now held a goodly part of Greece but not much else. Since Cassander had his hands full with bringing Macedon under his control, he was content to leave his rival be while he attempted diplomacy with the other successor generals.

The Wars in the East

In Asia Minor, Eumenes had his hands full as Antigonus demonstrated that age was no handicap to expert use of an army. Eumenes was pinned into the fortress of Nora in the Taurus Mountains, and was forced to swear an oath of allegiance to Antigonus. Plutarch in his *Life of Eumenes* argues that the canny general secretly changed the terms of the oath so as not to compromise his principles, but the basic fact is that he double-crossed Antigonus, escaped from Asia Minor and rebuilt an army loyal to Polyperchon in the east.

From there the war became a two-part affair. Events in the West have already been described. While Olympias and Cassander were fighting it out in Macedon, their struggle became ever more detached from that of Eumenes and Antigonus. Antigonus had the larger army, and he used it to drive Eumenes further and further east. Eumenes fought a skilful rearguard action, and easily held his own until the two sides met in 216 BC at a place called Gabiene in central Persia.

The main reason for Eumenes' unexpected military capability was that he retained command of the Silver Shields, the elite infantry unit of the Macedonian army. That unit was none too happy serving under a foreign commander, but the men fought well enough at Gabiene until they discovered that Antigonus had captured their camp. That camp contained not only the booty that this unit had accumulated over forty years of warfare, but the wives and children of the soldiers as well. The Silver Shields wanted their booty and families much more than they wanted Eumenes as a commander.

When offered a deal – their loot and families in exchange for Eumenes – the soldiers took it without hesitation. Eumenes was handed over to Antigonus who left his prisoner to survive without food for three days before he was executed. To make things even worse, Eumenes had not even been responsible for the loss of the baggage. That was due to an incompetent (or possibly treacherous) ally called Peucestas.

With the death of Eumenes, hostilities came to an end. However, with the end of the Second Successor War (319–315 BC) peace did not break out. Preparations to launch the sequel were already well under way. There was one reason for the Third Successor War, and that was Antigonus. Antigonus' feud with Eumenes had rampaged across the East from Asia Minor through Syria and into Persia. As Eumenes gave and Antigonus took land, Antigonus replaced satraps and realigned allegiances to suit himself. One victim of these re-dispositions was Seleucus, whom Antigonus casually kicked out of his position in Babylon, installing one of his own henchmen instead.

The indignant Seleucus fled to Ptolemy. Once there he explained that Antigonus now commanded the royal treasuries and the army of Eumenes. He was master of the empire from Anatolia and the Levant in the west all the way to Bactria 2,000 *stades* to the east. (ie 3,600km or 2,200 miles away). Apart from Ptolemy in Egypt, Cassander in Macedon, and a general called Lysimachus in Thrace, all of Alexander's massive empire was under the control of Antigonus and Demetrios, his son.

Unsurprisingly, this was unacceptable to the remaining Successors. They joined forces to issue an ultimatum. Either Antigonus voluntarily surrendered a substantial part of his lands and treasure, or he would be forced to surrender them involuntarily. Equally unsurprisingly, Antigonus informed the alliance that if they wanted what he had, they would have to fight for it.

The war developed on three fronts. Polyperchon promptly allied with Antigonus, on the basis that Cassander was against both of them. The beleaguered Antigonus took over operations in Asia Minor and the Levant and his son Demetrios took the rest of Syria and the task of containing Ptolemy in Egypt. Demetrios was famous for his extravagant lifestyle and his skill at storming cities (he is distinguished from the many other Demetri in history by the sobriquet 'Poliorcetes' – 'the Besieger'). Sadly for his father's cause, Demetrios was less good at defence than he was at attack, and he was soundly beaten by Ptolemy in Gaza. This allowed Seleucus to take a small corps of soldiers east and reclaim Babylonia – something he was only able to do because the Babylonians remembered his rule rather fondly, and certainly more fondly than that of his short-lived successor.

Antigonus had proven able to robustly defend his domains. Polyperchon had vigorously restarted his vendetta and was making life uncomfortable for Cassander, and Lysimachus suddenly found himself dealing with a host of rebellious Greek cities across his domains – mainly because Antigonus had offered to support their attempts for independence. Three years of indecisive fighting against Antigonus proved enough for Cassander and Lysimachus who now needed to tidy up at home. They opened negotiations with Antigonus and Ptolemy reluctantly went along with the peace deal.

Though the Third Successor War of 214–211 BC thus came to an end, the sequel had already begun. Antigonus had made peace with the other dynasts mainly because he also had some domestic housekeeping to do – the re-ejection of Seleucus from Babylonia.

The Babylonian War

Seleucus was not idle while Antigonus had been skirmishing with the other dynasts. He had strengthened his grip on Babylon and extended his grasp to take in several nearby kingdoms. Above all he had worked hard to recruit and train a handy little army. When the other dynasts made peace with Antigonus and left him in the lurch, it is improbable that Seleucus was surprised.

We know few details of what happened in Antigonus' war to evict Seleucus from Mesopotamia. The war is known as the Babylonian War, and it happened so far to the east that few later Greek historians took much interest in it. (This is a common issue with the history of the Hellenistic kingdoms. Despite the fact that almost half of Alexander's conquests were in the East, and included lands as rich and important as any to the west, the interest of later historians seems to have stopped dead at the banks of the River Euphrates. For the ethnocentric Greeks and Romans, what happened beyond the banks of that river was almost literally in another world.)

While we do not know the details of how Antigonus' invasion went, we do know that his army attacked in such overwhelming force that Seleucus was forced to give way. However, the canny general had prepared carefully for this event, and it proved remarkably difficult to nail him down in the countryside. A series of redoubts and hideaways in the southern marshes made it possible for even a substantial army to keep out of sight, so Seleucus was generally able to fight only when he chose to do so.

The situation in the West meant that Antigonus did not lead his army in person but had to leave the war to subordinates. These fared so badly that before long Seleucus had won several victories and control of the former Persian capital of Susa. This forced Antigonus to send his son to take charge of the campaign. This Demetrios did with the same marked lack of success as his predecessors. Even with fresh troops from the West he was unable to completely subdue Babylon. Finally Antigonus came to take charge of matters in person in 310 BC. This certainly broke the deadlock, because Seleucus decisively defeated Antigonus in battle the following year. This led, if not to a formal peace treaty, then to an agreed ceasefire.

Antiochus accepted that Babylonia was lost to him and pulled back to Syria. Seleucus in turn took his now-veteran army east. The Indian King Sandracottus (Chandragupta Maurya) had been harassing the satraps left behind to defend Alexander's eastern conquests. (Exactly who was doing what to whom is uncertain due to the lack of interest from contemporary sources.) Nevertheless it is clear that Seleucus, expecting further trouble from the West at any moment, was eager for a permanent settlement of the situation in the East. In the end Seleucus pragmatically gave up those of Alexander's conquests he did not feel were defensible, and in return Sandracottus gave Seleucus 500 war elephants.

(As an aside, in the conquests given up by Seleucus, the Indo-Greek fusion of cultures under Sandracottus' enlightened rule produced a successful and durable society which helped to take Sandracottus on to rule of one of the largest empires in Indian history.)

In his turn, Seleucus retained control of Bactria, Sogdiana and some north Indian territory. This meant that he now controlled the largest portion of Alexander's former domains – by area, if not by population.

The Babylonian War ended in 309 BC – not because peace broke out, but because the two sides stopped fighting each other. Two years later this stagnant conflict was subsumed into the more general conflagration of the Fourth Successor War.

The peace following the third Successor War had been enlivened by some military adventurism and double-cross on the part of the other Diadochi. Ptolemy had been building himself a navy, and now experimented with it by taking control of the island of Cyprus. Rather pleased with himself as leader of a naval power, Ptolemy went on the take the Aegean island of Kos and began to generally throw his weight about in the eastern Mediterranean. This included an abortive intervention in mainland Greece itself, much to the indignation of Cassander.

The End of Alexander's Line

Cassander's fury was understandable, because he felt he had just managed to get the Greek situation under control. Polyperchon was getting elderly, and had been handed a valuable bargaining chip in the person of Hercules – not the mythological hero but an alleged son of Alexander. There are legitimate grounds to doubt Hercules' parentage, in that the boy only made an appearance as a teen well after Alexander's death. However, his mother Barsine had undoubtedly shared Alexander's bed, so the boy had enough credibility to convince those who wanted to believe in his cause.

Antigonus sent the lad and his mother to Polyperchon in the hope that this 'son' of Alexander might rouse the Macedonian army to mutiny. Instead, Polyperchon used his new-found leverage to make peace. In exchange for continued control of southern Greece, Polyperchon surrendered his claims to the inheritance of Antipater. The deal with Cassander was sealed by the killing of Hercules and Barsine. Thereafter Polyperchon fades from the picture and probably died peacefully of old age in around 304 BC.

This left one survivor of the line of Alexander – his son by Roxana. This was Alexander IV, the legitimate ruler of the entire empire. Alexander was currently in Macedon under Cassander's 'protection'. Despite the various wars, land grabs and betrayals, all of the Diadochi still claimed to be acting as subordinates of the boy king – and the problem was that he would soon cease to be a boy. Once he passed the age of fourteen, Alexander IV could ditch his regents and start ruling in his own name.

Therefore we might assume that Antigonus might not have been completely unaware of what might happen when he handed Hercules to Polyperchon. With Hercules alive, the death of Alexander IV would mean that Hercules was the only possible inheritor to Alexander the Great's kingdom – and Hercules was in the power of Cassander's enemies.

The need to have Alexander IV around to counter-balance Hercules was mainly what was keeping the young king alive. Once Hercules was dead, Alexander IV was not necessary and was about to mature into a huge inconvenience. Therefore news was passed to the grieving Macedonian troops that both Alexander IV and Roxana had succumbed to illness – a claim which no-one believed for a moment. Because the actual killing was done in secrecy, the exact date of Alexander IV's demise is uncertain. While some historians argue that Alexander was killed before Hercules, it is unlikely that Cassander would have killed 'his' king while a rival claimant to the title was still alive.

Naval Warfare

Thus matters stood in 307 BC, when Antigonus returned to the West with his army. He was still smarting from his rough handling by Seleucus, and distinctly unimpressed with Ptolemy's adventurism in the Mediterranean. Furthermore, Polyperchon's grip on Greece was weakening and with the Greeks clearly unhappy at the prospect of direct rule by Cassander, Antigonus scented an opportunity to discomfit his rivals. He sent Demetrios to 'liberate' Athens from Macedonian rule – something the Athenians welcomed so enthusiastically that they literally deified Demetrios and set about building a navy which was to thereafter fight loyally for the Antigonid cause.

The purpose of the navy was to curb Ptolemy's maritime adventurism. Antigonus took exception to the assimilation of Cyprus into Ptolemy's domains, and anyway, Ptolemy seemed intent on provoking Antigonus further with naval raids along the coast of the Levant and Anatolia. The island of Rhodes, whose sailors were rivalled in seamanship only by the Athenians, was also inclining toward Ptolemy, so drastic action was required to stop the entire eastern Aegean from falling under Egyptian control.

Demetrios gathered both an army and a navy – the Rhodians declined to add their ships to the latter – and headed out to Cyprus. There he confronted the forces of Menelaus. (This Menelaus was the hitherto-unknown brother of Ptolemy, who only now makes an appearance on the stage of history.) While a relatively competent and dogged commander, neither Menelaus nor his army were a match for the greater numbers and experience which Demetrios brought to the confrontation. Menelaus was penned into the city of Cypriot Salamis (not to be confused with the more famous battle site near Athens), and Ptolemy was forced to hasten from Egypt in person to prevent his brother's imminent capture.

Ptolemy had a large force of around 200 triremes and quinqueremes (including those which Menelaus already had at Salamis), plus an army packed into a further 200 transports. Demetrios had about the same or slightly fewer warships, but around three dozen of these were crewed by highly-skilled Athenians. The battle was fought in 306 BC and was the largest naval action in the Aegean since the Peloponnesian War of a century previously. Demetrios took a personal part in the battle, fighting off a boarding party that attempted to take the flagship which he had led into the thick of the action. In the end Ptolemy was forced to withdraw with the loss of half his fleet. His remaining ships were unable to defend the transports, so as well as capturing some 40 warships which he repaired and re-purposed into his navy, Demetrios picked up a handy 6,000 or so prisoners, who promptly joined his army.

So exuberant did this success make Demetrios that upon the now-inevitable surrender of Menelaus, the victor was decidedly generous. Menelaus was allowed to take himself, his friends, and all his personal possessions back to Egypt. There his cameo appearance ends, and Menelaus once again disappears into obscurity.

This victory of his son meant that Cyprus now fell to Antigonus, along with the remainder of the Ptolemaic army which had been garrisoning the island. Combined with news of the death of Hercules and Alexander IV, this inspired Antigonus to proclaim himself as king. Certainly Antigonus was now the richest and most powerful of the Diadochi, but this did not mean that the others were prepared to accept his suzerainty. In short order, Seleucus, Cassander, Ptolemy and Lysimachus of Thrace crowned themselves as kings also. The empire of Alexander was now formally broken up, never again to be reunited.

Chapter 5

Wars of the Successors – Part II

By now it was clear to the other Diadochi that Antigonus represented an existential threat. Firstly, a part the kingdom of Antigonus abutted the realm of each of the other Successors, making the invasion of their territory relatively straightforward. Secondly, Antigonus had a large and experienced army with which to do the invading. Thirdly, because he occupied the richest parts of the former Persian Empire, Antigonus had the money to pay those troops and to raise more if need be. Finally, there could be no question of waiting for old age to carry away the 78-year-old veteran and the threat he represented. In the wings to succeed him was the younger, more erratic but undoubtedly competent Demetrios.

It was an interesting question as to whether Antigonus alone was now more powerful than the other Successors combined. The only way to answer that question was for the other Successors to combine forces, and herding cats was far easier than forcing these very diverse and independent rulers to collaborate on anything. Nevertheless, Antigonus seemed determined to make them try.

The one exception to the individualism of the Diadochi was Seleucus, who was eager to ally with anyone who was offering. Seleucus was close to the top of Antigonus' 'to-do' list, and he knew it. He had already once had to fight off Antigonid armies without help, and he was not eager to have to do it again.

After Seleucus' experience in Babylonia, the next to receive a salutary scare was Ptolemy. Antigonus reckoned that the loss of much of the Egyptian fleet and army had weakened Ptolemy both in terms of military strength and political prestige. Therefore the next logical step was to invade Egypt and see if Ptolemy could be evicted from that ancient kingdom before he could recover his strength.

The invasion came hard on the heels of the capture of Cyprus, late in 306 BC. Antigonus did not want to give Ptolemy the winter to rally political support and train new troops. Therefore he gambled on winter storms holding off long enough for him to gain a secure beachhead in Egypt before the weather closed the seas to shipping. The sea was needed because Antigonus did not have time to force his way through Gaza with slow sieges. The plan was to land the army behind the Gaza strongpoints and then supply the field army by sea. If Egypt fell then Gaza would automatically fall into Antigonus' power in any case.

By any count this was a risky strategy, but Antigonus had not reached his present power by playing safe. At worst, Antigonus reckoned, even if Demetrios could not get enough supplies to him to sustain a campaign, at some point the weather would break long enough for the army to be evacuated back to Syria. As it turned out, that is exactly what happened. Militarily this was merely a setback. Politically the damage was greater. Ptolemy now shared the opinion of Seleucus that even Alexander's massive domains were not big enough to hold both himself and Antigonus. He and Seleucus – the pair of whom had always been on friendly terms anyway – began to cautiously sound out the others about an anti-Antigonus alliance. This coalition of the willing was given a field trial in the Aegean, where Antigonus had decided that the island of Rhodes needed to be punished for its sympathy for Ptolemy.

The other Successors poured expert builders, skilled manpower and money into Rhodes before the island was closed to the outside world by the arrival of Demetrios and a substantial fleet. An epic siege followed. At one point Antigonid forces breached the walls of the city, but they were forced out and the walls repaired. For the siege Demetrios built a massive siege engine half the height of a skyscraper. (Literally. A modern skyscraper must be a minimum of 80 metres tall. Demetrios' machine was over 40 metres and at least six stories tall – and it was mobile.)

Even this monster was insufficient to overcome the dogged resistance of the Rhodians. Nor was there available the option of starving the islanders into submission. The nimble Rhodian sea craft and their expert crews thumbed their noses at the warships of Demetrios which tried unsuccessfully to close them off from the sea lanes. In the end, with his men growing restless and the Antigonid prestige ebbing more by the day,

Demetrios arranged a face-saving compromise. In return for peace, the Rhodians agreed to renounce any potential alliance with Ptolemy and sit out the war between the two Successors, a war which was currently in abeyance but still a going concern.

A notable side effect of the siege of Rhodes was how the islanders decided to dispose of the remnants of the huge siege tower of Demetrios and the other detritus of war that littered the island. The famous designer and architect called Chares of Lindos was asked if he could use the raw material to make a commemorative statue 35 cubits (around 15 metres) in height. The story goes that Chares agreed to the commission. Then he was asked if he could double the height of the statue. Chares agreed to do this for double the cost.

Regrettably, as Chares should have known, building does not work that way. For example, a concrete support 8 inches in diameter weighs 52 pounds. Double that up to support a statue twice the size, and the weight rises to 200 pounds. Double the lower tiers again to support that load and suddenly we have gone from 8 inches at 52 pounds to 36 inches at well over 1,000 pounds. Faced with exponentially rising building costs, Chares allegedly committed suicide.

Still, he might have considered his sacrifice worthwhile, for the statue became instantly famous. Known as the Colossus of Rhodes, the epic memorial quickly became one of the seven wonders of the ancient world. It was perhaps the least durable of the seven wonders, for it lasted a mere half century before being toppled by an earthquake. (In contrast the oldest wonder – the Great Pyramid at Giza – is still going strong after 4,500 years.) Nevertheless, the Colossus marks the first flowering of the development in architecture, art and invention which defines the Hellenistic era.

Showdown at Ipsus, 301 BC

Rebuffed at Rhodes, Demetrios went to take out his bad temper on Cassander. The two Diadochi had been on bad terms ever since Demetrios' takeover of Athens, and relations had not been improved by Cassander's substantial aid to the Rhodians during the failed siege of the previous year. (Ptolemy, typically, upstaged Cassander by awarding himself the title of *soter* or 'saviour' for the help he had given the Rhodians in that same siege.)

Cassander found himself unable to withstand the formidable Demetrios and his battle-hardened army, and only the natural defences of Macedonia allowed him to hold on to the heartlands of his kingdom after defeat in Greece. Cassander sent ambassadors seeking peace, but it appeared that Antigonus was intent on adding Greece and Macedon to his domains. The Macedonian envoys were rebuffed.

Seleucus and Ptolemy were already on the anti-Antigonus bandwagon, and Demetrios had now practically shoved Cassander aboard. That left Lysimachus of Thrace. Under similar circumstances a few millennia later, Benjamin Franklin would remark 'Gentlemen, we must all hang together, or we shall undoubtedly hang separately'. Lysimachus accepted that he either joined the coalition against Antigonus now, or he would have to face Antigonus alone later. Accordingly he girded his loins, mustered his army, and invaded Anatolia.

Antigonus mustered an army of his own and came to meet Lysimachus. Probably wisely, Lysimachus declined to confront the veteran general until he had help, and the remainder of the year saw a cat-and-mouse game played out in Asia Minor. Antigonus constantly attacked Lysimachus, attempting to force him from his camp entrenchments. When he came close to succeeding through use of artillery and siege works, Lysimachus – not without difficulty – would shift camps. The object of the delay was for Lysimachus to hold out until the arrival of Seleucus. That general had left his domains post-haste at the news of Lysimachus' invasion of Asia Minor, but the sheer size of the Hellenistic conquests meant that, even moving at the trot, it took an army at least three months to get from Babylonia to Asia Minor.

Once word reached Antigonus that Seleucus was on his way, Antigonus recalled Demetrios from Greece. At this point Demetrios had forced his way into Thessaly and was tangling unproductively with the army of Cassander. When the summons arrived, Demetrios patched up an ad-hoc ceasefire with Cassander which enabled him to get his troops to Asia Minor. (Cassander attempted to send his own army after Demetrios, but the attempt to join forces with Lysimachus was largely foiled by bad weather and the vigilance of Demetrios.)

However, Demetrios could do nothing about the opportunistic Ptolemy. As soon as he heard of events to the north, Ptolemy came storming out of Egypt, intent on capturing and fortifying as much of Syria as he could lay hands on. It was rather typical of the cautious Ptolemy that he retreated back to Egypt as soon as he received news that Antigonus had defeated the allies in the north. As it turned out, the news was both premature and wrong. Antigonus had not yet engaged the alliance, and was still campaigning in Anatolia. One suspects that the reports received by Ptolemy were fake news generated by the Antagonids, for Ptolemy's retreat meant that there was one less of the Diadochi on the battlefield when the eventual showdown did arrive.

Our knowledge of what happened next becomes somewhat more sketchy, for at this point the *History* of Cassius Dio survives in only fragmentary form. This forces us to fall back on the unwarlike Plutarch, who gives an account of the climactic battle in his *Life of Demetrios*. As Plutarch concentrates on the human interest aspect, a number of technical details have gone missing. We know what mood the father-and-son pair shared before the battle (thoughtful and subdued) but nothing of the pre-battle manoeuvres or initial deployments. We know that the battle was fought at Ipsus, but it would have been nice of Plutarch to tell us where Ipsus was. All we know for certain is that it was somewhere in Phrygia in northwestern Anatolia.

This battle was to decide who ruled the Hellenistic east. As Plutarch points out, this would have already been Antigonus had he shown the slightest inclination toward diplomacy. Even accommodating one of the Diadochi (Seleucus would have been an obvious choice) would have so weakened the others that Antigonus would have been beyond challenge. As it was, things had come to this – an all-or-nothing confrontation between Antigonus and the combined strength of the others.

Even then, Antigonus came close to victory. His son Demetrios charged down from the Antigonid right wing with superior cavalry, and quickly routed the enemy horse before him. Next, Demetrios should have swept around the back of the allied phalanx or attempted to engage the enemy's horse on the other wing. (In a traditional phalanx battle the strongest cavalry force was positioned on the right wing of each army.) Instead, true to his impetuous nature, Demetrios pushed further than he should have done in pursuit of the cavalry he had defeated, and thus separated himself from the rest of the Antigonid army.

This was a fatal mistake. Seleucus had not contributed many men to the coalition's forces, but he had brought 400 of the war elephants which he had obtained in India as part of his settlement with Sandracottus. Now, with great tactical awareness, Seleucus threw his elephants into a battle line which cut Demetrios off from the Antigonid phalanx. It is a mystery where the elephants had been stationed up to this point, since it is hard to imagine a useful deployment which would allow them to be repositioned so handily. Either the elephants had been kept in reserve – unheard-of and not very useful since elephants were normally shock troops – or Seleucus had foreseen with unusual prescience how the cavalry action would go and had gambled accordingly with his deployment.

However they got there, the elephants were highly effective when they arrived. Plutarch makes much of the fact that the cavalry horses were unused to elephants and so disturbed by the noises and smells that they refused to go near them. This may be something of an exaggeration, because Antigonus did have elephants of his own, though far fewer of them. Nevertheless, the fact is that Demetrios was unable to break through the elephantine barrier and rejoin the battle.

This tipped the scales in the coalition's favour. Seleucus pushed back the remainder of the Antigonid cavalry with his own horsemen. Then he did as Demetrios should have done and rode around the back of the Antigonid phalanx. The depth of that phalanx is unknown, but the more shallow the deployment, the harder it would have been for the back ranks to disengage and face the new threat. Seleucus did not charge, but he kept threatening to do so, causing consternation and disruption in the ranks of his opponents. At the same time it is probable that his light cavalry ranged to and fro across the back of the phalanx discharging missiles and javelins into the tight-packed mass of men.

Although Plutarch does not say so explicitly, we can assume that by now the Antigonid phalanx had engaged with that of the alliance, and that an infantry battle was being waged simultaneously to the ructions in the rear ranks. If so, it was hardly a formula for an Antigonid victory. The only thing holding the phalanx together was the leadership of Antigonus himself, who insisted that Demetrios would return in time to save the day.

That was not to be. The phalanx was crumbling, with large numbers switching sides to join the obvious victor. A squad of javelineers was dispatched against the king. 'While he was still watching eagerly for his son, a cloud of javelins enveloped him, and he fell.' (Plutarch *Demetrios*)

The end of Antigonus brought about the end of the Battle of Ipsus which resulted in the end of the Antigonid Empire. Demetrios fled with enough men to be a considerable nuisance for years to come, but he would never come close to recovering his father's domains. Those domains were carved up by the victors 'as though they were a monstrous carcass', Plutarch reports.

Aftermath

The last chance to reunite Alexander's empire fell with Antigonus at Ipsus, but it is doubtful that such an empire could have survived in any case. The whole thing was simply too large and diverse for any one ruler to manage. The largest of the kingdoms to emerge from the break-up was that of Seleucus – and even that proved too large to be manageable. The Hellenistic world was centred on the Mediterranean, which inevitably meant that the focus of the Seleucid kings was on the West. The Bactrians, Indians and others on the eastern fringes of the empire began to drift away from the empire almost from the time of conquest, without their rulers paying a great deal of attention to their going.

Probably the big winner from the Battle of Ipsus was Ptolemy, for all that he had refrained from striking a blow. Though news of a supposed Antigonid advance had sent him hurrying back to Egypt, Ptolemy had left behind him a large number of garrisoned cities and strongpoints which he had no intention of handing over. Northern Syria and points east fell to Seleucus. However, Seleucus felt – with some justification – that southern Syria and the Levant should also belong to him. Ptolemy felt equally strongly that they shouldn't. This disagreement was never resolved, and for almost the rest of the Hellenic era the Ptolemaic and Seleucid kings would butt heads over the region in a series of ultimately futile wars.

Directly after Ipsus, Seleucus did not have an army strong enough to dispute Ptolemy's *de facto* control of southern Syria. Nor did he have the time, for he had a new empire to settle down and organize. Furthermore, though the borders of his own and Ptolemy's domains were now more or less settled, matters to the west remained in flux, and Seleucus had to keep up his guard for trouble from that direction.

For a start, Demetrios had no intention of retiring quietly into obscurity. By way of revenge on Lysimachus, Demetrios and the remnants of his army rampaged through the Thracian Chersonese. Demetrios remained allies with the skilled and opportunistic Pyrrhus of Epirus, an alliance based on the rough understanding that Pyrrhus would be allowed as much of Greece as he could take while Demetrios set his sights on Macedon. This aggression by Demetrios rather undid everything which Cassander had gained from the fall of Antigonus, as he had mostly wanted to get Demetrios off his back in the first place. It did not help that Cassander was now very ill and his sons had become bitter rivals over the succession.

Meanwhile, in Asia Minor Lysimachus had decided that the possessions of Seleucus were far too extensive, and his own were far too meagre relative to the part he had played in the overthrow of Antigonus. Accordingly Lysimachus began to seize what lands he could in Asia Minor. He was aided in this by Ptolemy who saw in Lysimachus a valuable distraction which would prevent Seleucus from exercising his grievances about southern Syria.

So strongly did Ptolemy support Lysimachus that he gave to him his daughter Arsinoe in marriage. (Like Cleopatra and Eurydice, Arsinoe was one of a small number of names shared by almost all Hellenistic queens, so keeping track of which Arsinoe was married to whom is one of the challenges for historians of the period. For example, at the time of this marriage Lysimachus had a son and two daughters from an earlier marriage. The daughters were called Eurydice and Arsinoe.)

Though the Ptolemaic marriage came with a valuable diplomatic connection, it is fairly certain that Lysimachus preferred the diplomatic connection to the girl who came with it. Arsinoe was at this time in her early teens (Lysimachus was in his 60s) and a very strong-willed character. Nor could Lysimachus rein her in without upsetting Ptolemy, so domestic relations in the palace became severely strained.

Matters took another turn in 297 BC when Cassander died. In the dynastic struggle for Macedon which followed, one son died, and a second drove out the third. The exiled son turned to Demetrios for support. This was effective but unwise. Demetrios did indeed secure the kingdom, but he then killed the son and set himself up as Demetrios I of Macedon. Demetrios had a sort of husbandly claim to the throne, because his wife was the sister of Cassander and the daughter of Antipater, Alexander's former regent in Macedon. Thus Demetrios could claim that he was actually keeping the throne warm for his son (also called Antigonus), who was of the actual royal bloodline through his mother.

The Macedonians had on their eastern flank the hostile Lysimachus, who regarded Demetrios as unfinished business left over from the Battle of Ipsus. In the west was the opportunistic Pyrrhus, who had no claim to the throne of Macedon, but wanted it nevertheless. Southern Greece was highly unsettled. For Macedon and Demetrios, the coming decades were going to be turbulent.

The New World Order – Ptolemy digs in

The main advantage which Ptolemy enjoyed over the other Diadochi was that he knew exactly what he wanted. That was basically Egypt. In Ptolemy's mind Egypt also included the land of Cyrenaica to the west. Cyrenaica was valuable because of the Pentopolis, a grouping of five large Greek cities which had been there since around the sixth century BC. These combined with Greek settlements in Egypt such as Naucratis to give a Greek flavour to an otherwise-alien kingdom. On the other hand, the Greeks of Cyrenaica were decidedly unenthusiastic about coming under Egyptian rule, and it was only in 300 BC, after a series of rebellions, that the promise of limited autonomy reconciled them – grudgingly – to Ptolemaic rule. Thereafter, Ptolemy used his currently unemployed army and the disarray of the other Diadochi to reclaim Cyprus in 295 BC.

Ptolemy regarded Cyprus as he did southern Syria – less an integral part of his kingdom, and more of a frontier buffer. Fortified and garrisoned strongpoints in Syria needed to be overcome before any land attack could be mounted on Egypt proper. Any attack on Egypt by sea would have ships from Cyprus and friendly Rhodes sitting across the attacker's supply lines. Getting past these obstacles would be time-consuming for an enemy, and the delay would give Ptolemy time to prepare the defence of his heartlands.

As well as a defensive role, Cyprus was ideally positioned for raids aimed at causing trouble in southern Anatolia in general and Caria in particular. (In fact so successful were those raids that Ptolemy managed to seize and hold a considerable chunk of territory on the mainland.) Also, while not ideal, Cyprus was a useful forward base for making life awkward for whoever held Greece. Ships from Cyprus could bring money, men and logistical support for rebels in mainland Greece more easily than could transport from the Nile Delta itself.

Thereafter, Ptolemy concentrated his efforts on diplomacy, mostly conducted through a host of nubile daughters. We have already seen that Ptolemy secured an alliance with Lysimachus by giving him his daughter Arsinoe in marriage. A step-daughter was married to secure an alliance with Syracuse, and in 296 BC Ptolemy signalled a desire to be reconciled with Demetrios by betrothing his daughter Ptolemais.

Overall then, Ptolemy was on equable terms with all the Diadochi. Seleucus was still simmering about Ptolemy's annexation of southern Syria, but the pair were still officially allies. Furthermore Seleucus was indebted to Ptolemy for earlier having helped him to gain control of Babylonia. Lysimachus was now a son-in-law by marriage, as was Demetrios. Cassander was now out of the picture, and with Demetrios in command of Macedon, Cassander's surviving son had become irrelevant. Ptolemy was at peace with the world, and prepared to settle down to a quiet retirement preparing his memoirs. Historians would love to unearth a copy of the *Campaigns of Alexander*, which Ptolemy wrote at this point, but sadly the manuscript has not survived.

Seleucus consolidates

In Syria, Seleucus was working hard to remedy what he saw as the major weakness of his kingdom – a lack of Greeks. One feature common to all of Alexander's successors is that they failed to share Alexander's vision of combining Greek and Eastern cultures. Instead they took the 'Hellenistic' part of their kingdoms very seriously and endeavoured to attract as many Greeks as possible to their domains.

Rather than work out how trade and manufacturing had been conducted in the region for millennia, the Diadochi showed a preference for importing people who did it in a manner which they already understood. Also, having beaten the Persians and their subjects in war, Alexander's successors definitely preferred to have Greek troops in their army. This was particularly true of Seleucus, Ptolemy and their successors. Well aware that they were non-native rulers, these monarchs realized that if they armed and trained native troops then those same troops might rebel against their foreign overlords.

Since classical Greece was an urban culture, Seleucus aimed to attract Greek immigrants by building cities. The first of these was built in Babylonia, his old centre of power. Seleucus named the new city Seleucia after himself, and built it 30 kilometres further down the River Tigris from Babylon itself.

The Babylonians were understandably unhappy at having a rival city built so close nearby and were worried about losing population and prestige to the new foundation. (Rightly as it turned out – the decline of Babylon as one of the world's great cities becomes pronounced soon after Seleucia became a major urban centre.) There is a story that Babylonian astrologers deliberately gave Seleucus an inauspicious date on which to begin construction, but the soldiers and workmen spontaneously began building at a more propitious time. A more cynical observer might assume that Seleucus was tipped off about the Babylonian shenanigans, but he did not want to upset the Babylonians more than necessary by openly flouting the 'official' start date.

Seleucia – named Seleucia-on-the-Tigris to distinguish it from the other eight Seleucias which were founded during the reign of Seleucus – was to grow to become one of the great cities of the Hellenic world. The later Roman writer Pliny the Elder put the population at well over half a million people, and though some of these came from Babylon and Mesopotamia, many others were the Greek immigrants whom Seleucus was seeking.

Another major foundation was Antioch on the River Orontes between Anatolia and Syria. It is probable that this city was started by Antigonus

Monophthalmus. After the city fell to Seleucus as a result of the victory at Ipsus, the city underwent a name adjustment from Antigonea to Antioch – Antiochus being a traditional Seleucid family name shared by both the father and son of Seleucus, and many others later.

There were numerous other city foundations, including over a dozen more Antiochs, but these two cities became the twin centres of the new Seleucid Empire. Antioch was the western base, and Seleucia controlled Mesopotamia and points east.

Those 'points east' meant especially Bactria and neighbouring Sogdiana. Both these areas had a pronounced Greek presence, but they were always the high-tide mark of Hellenism, isolated from the mainstream of Greek culture. During the wars of the Diadochi the province was under the capable rule of a former subordinate of Alexander called Stasanor. Stasanor kept the province peaceful and out of the fighting in the west. Nevertheless, because the dominant power in the west was Antigonus, Stasanor accepted him as his nominal overlord. This was unacceptable to Seleucus who launched a brisk attack to depose him immediately after the Babylonian war of 305 BC.

Seleucus had Bactria administered by his son Antiochus, who was Sogdianan on his mother's side. Antiochus was sent to run the eastern empire after one of these rather disturbing family incidents which are a hallmark of the Hellenistic kings. The story goes that one day young Antiochus went off his food. From being merely pale and interesting he went on to become downright ill from self-neglect. His alarmed father eventually traced the reason for his son's decline to a passionate love for his stepmother, Stratonice. After a quick check with Stratonice's father Demetrios (the Successors were attempting to play nice with each other at this point and dynastic intermarriage was the norm), Seleucus divorced Stratonice who married Antiochus. Since Seleucus was much more elderly than Stratonice, the new marriage to his son was more age-appropriate in any case.

The next generation

Cassander was already out of the picture. The end of the decade of the 280s BC would see also the end of the remaining Diadochi. Demetrios was the first to get into trouble. His infamously decadent lifestyle upset and angered the rather strait-laced Macedonians, and his inability to protect his kingdom from the increasingly predatory raids of Pyrrhus of Epirus was a major irritant. In 288 BC matters came to a head. Athens rebelled with the support of all the other Diadochi – and when Demetrios went south to deal with the problem, the Macedonians closed ranks behind him, and firmly assured their king that they did not want him back. Unwanted in Greece, Demetrios attempted to fight his way into Asia Minor, where he hoped that the continuing friction between Lysimachus and Seleucus might offer him a toehold. Instead, defeated and largely abandoned by his men, Demetrios ended as a prisoner of Seleucus.

Macedon passed to Demetrios' son. In his calm competence this son resembled his grandfather, Antipater, who had administered Macedon while Alexander was away conquering the world. Distinguished from many later Antigonids by the additional appellation of 'Gonatas', this Antigonus offered ever-higher ransoms in an attempt to persuade Seleucus to part with his father. Seleucus was unyielding, and Demetrios was dead three years later.

Rather than poison his inconvenient captive, it seems that Seleucus simply left Demetrios to kill himself through overindulgence. Plutarch remarks sardonically that Demetrios had raised armies and conquered provinces so that he could live in idleness and luxury on the spoils. Yet ironically it was only after he had lost everything that Demetrios was able to throw himself whole-heartedly into the dissipation he desired, but which led to his death.

> *Through folly and empty ambition which brought many troubles upon himself and upon others. What he had sought with weapons, fleets and armies he now, to his surprise, discovered in idleness and leisure.*
>
> (Plutarch *Demetrios* 52)

Next to go was Ptolemy, who, like Demetrios, died in bed with his boots off, though unlike the 54-year-old Demetrios he died at the ripe old age of 84. Ptolemy left a tidy kingdom with a well-organized dynastic succession. Ptolemy had decided earlier that his eldest son Ptolemy was unsuitable for the throne, and had therefore repudiated him in favour of his son Ptolemy.

(In order to navigate this abundance of Ptolemies, additional appellations are used by historians both ancient and modern. So the above sentence should read 'Ptolemy I Soter had decided earlier that his eldest son Ptolemy Keraunos was unsuitable for the throne, and had therefore repudiated him in favour of his younger son Ptolemy II Philadelphus.')

At this point it is necessary to digress into the domestic arrangements of the Hellenistic kings. This as we have already seen, is a world where all the protagonists knew each other. Even if they did not like each other, the kings constantly intermarried, because it cemented diplomatic alliances and gave the bloodlines of their offspring greater legitimacy. However, with members of the royal families, familiarity (sometimes familiarity to the point of incest) certainly bred contempt. It also bred rivalry, palace intrigue, backstabbing, double cross and the liberal use of poison.

Thus when Ptolemy Keraunos was tossed from the Egyptian succession, he took himself to the Thracian kingdom of Lysimachus. There he had a number of family connections. His mother, Eurydice was the daughter of Lysimachus' old commander, Antipater of Macedon. Lysimachus was too distracted to do much with the new arrival, because his young wife Arsinoe was furiously conspiring to get her children put ahead of Lysimachus' current heir, Agathocles, whose mother was another daughter of Antipater's called Nicaea (and therefore the maternal aunt of Ptolemy Keraunos).

Ptolemy Keraunos pitched into the palace intrigues on the side of Agathocles, because Lysandra, the wife of Agathocles, was his sister. Her rival Arsinoe was also a half-sister, but the full sister of Ptolemy Philadelphus, the hated half-brother who had replaced Ptolemy Keraunos as heir to the Egyptian throne.

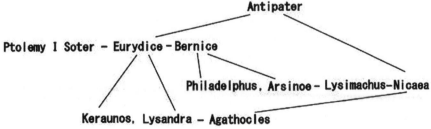

Simplified family chart. Horizontal bar = married. Comma = siblings. Other lines show children.

As it turned out, Arsinoe persuaded Lysimachus that Agathocles had become treasonous and was attempting to poison their son (named Ptolemy, naturally). Agathocles was duly executed and Keraunos and Lysandra fled to Seleucus for protection. This Seleucus was more than happy to provide. He and Lysimachus had ganged up on Demetrios when that king tried to invade Asia Minor, but the underlying tension between the pair had never been fully resolved. With the execution of the popular Agathocles, Seleucus reckoned that the morale of the army of the ageing Lysimachus was low enough for it to be worth gambling a battle. Accordingly Seleucus marched his army into Asia Minor and challenged Lysimachus to defend his possessions.

The final confrontation between the last generals of Alexander was fought in 281 BC, in western Anatolia near the old Persian capital of Sardis. Lysimachus, who like the other Diadochi was now in his eighties, lost the battle and his life. This final victory meant that Seleucus had outlived – among others – Perdiccas, Cassander, Ptolemy, Eumenes, Lysimachus, Antigonus, Demetrios, Alexander IV and Philip Arrhidaeus. He was now master of Macedon (Antigonus Gonatas was still fighting, but confined to a few strongpoints), Thrace, and all the remainder of Alexander's empire except Egypt. Not bad going for someone who started after Alexander's death as commander of the cavalry.

Now all that remained to be done was for Seleucus to return west to claim Lysimachus' European possessions. Then, apart from the outstanding matter of Egypt, the reunification of the empire – which had come close to happening under Antigonus Monophthalmus – would finally take place under Seleucus.

It should be noted that the Fates had made plain their opposition to this idea. When – as was usual for any Greek contemplating a journey – Seleucus had asked an oracle whether he would have a safe trip, the oracle unambiguously replied 'Stay in Asia'. Despite this, Seleucus did the trip. He may perhaps have been inspired by a desire to revisit as a conquering king the homeland he had last seen as an ambitious young man.

Regrettably, Seleucus chose an even more ambitious young man to accompany him on his homecoming. This was young Ptolemy Keraunos who, once they were on European soil, suggested that the pair should visit an isolated shrine and there thank the gods for the successful outcome of events. At the shrine Seleucus was briefly separated from his bodyguards. Keraunos took the opportunity to murder the benefactor who had taken him in and avenged the death of his brother-in-law. Keraunos' motive was simple. Once Seleucus was dead then, the claims of Antigonus Gonatas aside, Keraunos was next in line for the Macedonian throne. This situation might change if the elderly Seleucus were to live much longer, so Keraunos saw his chance and struck as swiftly as the thunderbolt after which he was named. (Keraunos means 'thunderbolt'.) Even at the time, it was uncertain whether the murder was premeditated, or if Keraunos suddenly saw an opportunity, and spontaneously seized it with amoral pragmatism.

The end of an era

The death of Seleucus saw the passing of the last of the generals who had been with Alexander through his conquests. When Seleucus was born, the East was divided into the Greek world and the mighty Persian Empire – though there was considerable overlap between the two in Anatolia. After Alexander's conquests and death, the Persian Empire had vanished and the Greek world had both massively expanded and been riven by instability and almost non-stop conflict.

Alexander's conquests stopped with Alexander. The Greek world would never again be as large as it was on his death in Babylon in 323 BC. In fact, that world almost immediately began to contract as the Successors realized that Alexander's Indian conquests could not be sustained militarily, lying as they did at the end of a 3,000 mile-long supply chain.

The wars which the Successors fought for Alexander's legacy were utterly bereft of idealism. The Diadochi were not fighting for different visions of what they thought Alexander's empire should become, but simply for as much of that empire as they could grab for themselves. The reward for victory was land and power, not the triumph of a particular ideology. It was purely and simply a struggle for supremacy among the most powerful, and a struggle for survival for those lower down the food chain.

While some of the measures taken by the Diadochi had indeed benefited the lives of their subjects, those benefits were secondary objectives. Thriving cities produced soldiers, and a strong economy meant that soldiers could be paid. Farms produced food to feed the army. A happy populace was less likely to erupt into distracting rebellions. The fact that what was good for the Hellenistic kings was often good also for their subjects was basically a happy coincidence.

In later years the philosophically-inclined Antigonus Gonatas was to come up with the theory that a king existed to serve his people. Such an idea was alien to the Diadochi, who considered that things worked the opposite way around – the people of their kingdoms existed as the support structure for their armies, since without those armies there would be no kingdom in the first place.

This changed to some extent when the heirs to the Diadochi took over. The men of this second generation were not particularly interested in securing for themselves lands they had never possessed and which were alien to them in any case. Rather they were intent on securing and consolidating what they already had, and for the reasons mentioned above, thriving and contented populations were the best means to that end. Therefore warfare became less intense, and (relatively) stable borders evolved between kingdoms which had previously been swapped between the Diadochi as their fortunes waxed and waned.

With the death of Lysimachus his kingdom had largely dissolved, and its component parts were assimilated into the domains of the neighbours. The Seleucids laid claim to those parts in Asia Minor, though they never really succeeded in making good on those claims, and the Macedonians aimed at securing those parts of Lysimachus' kingdom which lay on the European side.

After this, while there was to be considerable warfare and rivalry for the remainder of the Hellenistic era, the Greek world settled down into three kingdoms, each very different, but with a shared culture among the ruling class. These kingdoms were the Egypt of Ptolemy II, the Seleucid Empire of Antiochus, and the Kingdom of Macedon, which – despite the best efforts of Ptolemy Keraunos to secure himself on the throne – was still up for grabs.

Each kingdom faced different challenges. The Ptolemies had to show that they could become acceptable to their Egyptian subjects in a way that the Persians before them had never been. The Seleucids had to control an empire which was practically ungovernable simply due to its immense size – quite apart from the huge diversity of the peoples within it (more than sixty languages were spoken in Anatolia alone). Macedon faced the same challenges as that kingdom always had: hordes of barbarian invaders from the north and the restive and unruly Greek states to the south. The main difference was that there were now far fewer Macedonians to meet those barbarian hordes. Tens of thousands of Macedonians had already moved to the new lands of opportunity which had opened up in the East.

Chapter 6

Hellenism: the Next Generation

Antigonus Gonatas in Macedon

In the years after the death of Seleucus, Macedon was the most troubled part of the Greek world. There Ptolemy Keraunos found that seizing the kingdom was a lot easier than actually ruling it. To further legitimize his claim to the throne, Keraunos managed to lay hands on Arsinoe, the widow of the defeated Lysimachus, as she attempted to flee to the south. 'Lay hands on' was no metaphor for, half-sister or no, Ptolemy had determined on making Arsinoe his wife.

The blushing bride was deeply unhappy with this arrangement, and immediately set about employing her talent for palace intrigue against her new husband. She had a reasonably free hand to do this, for Keraunos was necessarily preoccupied by the intensifying barbarian pressure on the northern frontier. This pressure pre-dated Keraunos' seizure of the throne. In earlier years Lysimachus had also been forced to campaign against the invaders. (Not that these campaigns were successful. Either Lysimachus, or Agathocles, or both – the sources are unclear – had been captured but later released by the barbarian king.) Since no Macedonian army would accept a king who remained idle in the face of a barbarian threat, Keraunos was forced to take the field, while leaving spies to keep as careful a watch as possible on events back home at the palace.

In due course messengers reached Keraunos with news that, thanks to wifely plotting, a coup was indeed imminent. The king had to hurry back to his capital and, indeed, use his army to force entry into the city. Arsinoe cut her losses and fled, as did her eldest son. However, so precipitately was Arsinoe forced to flee that she had to leave her two younger children behind. These royal heirs were promptly killed by the vengeful Keraunos.

The departure of his scheming ex-wife (her flight was interpreted as a unilateral declaration of divorce) left Keraunos free to return to the barbarian threat, which in 279 BC became a great deal more severe. The kingdom now faced a huge incursion by a Gallic tribe called the Galatians, and the battered Macedonian army was in no shape to face a threat so severe. Ptolemy and his men were steamrollered by the barbarian marauders who thereafter rampaged through Macedonia and went on to plunder southern Greece, including the sacred treasuries at Delphi.

Ptolemy Keraunos died in that first Galatian onslaught. This left only one survivor among the many who had claimed the Macedonian throne in the previous two decades. That was Antigonus Gonatas, the son of Demetrios. While Gonatas was the only serious candidate for the Macedonian throne, there was little enough Macedon left after the Galatians had pillaged their way through the place. It took two years for the Greeks to fight off the invaders, and when the Galatians were thrown back, they retreated towards Macedonia.

This time Gonatas was ready, and the Galatians were decisively beaten in 277 BC at something between a battle and a massive ambush. With victory giving him further legitimacy, Gonatas formally claimed the Macedonian throne that year. As a bonus, his wife gave birth to the son who was to become Demetrios II of Macedon. Rebuilding the kingdom began, but the project was almost immediately interrupted by Pyrrhus of Epirus.

Pyrrhus had been a constant thorn in Macedon's side for years. A decade previously Pyrrhus, together with Lysimachus, had taken over Macedonia when Gonatas' father Demetrios had been driven out. Lysimachus had little patience with Pyrrhus, and soon kicked the Epirot army out of Macedon and incorporated the kingdom with his Thracian domains. Thereafter, Pyrrhus left Macedon to its troubles and went west in an attempt to defeat the nascent empire of Rome.

Pyrrhus won his battles in Italy, but these were so expensive in terms of money and manpower that after one such clash he complained, 'Another victory like that and I shall be ruined' – the origin of the term 'Pyrrhic victory'. Ultimately, Pyrrhus' campaign in Italy achieved nothing except to inculcate into the Romans a deep-seated fear of a further invasion from the Hellenic kingdoms – a fear which was to translate into pre-emptive action a century later.

On returning from his Italian adventure, Pyrrhus reinforced his army with Gallic mercenaries – possibly including leftovers from the Galatian onslaught. (The remainder of that Galatian invasion ricocheted around the eastern Mediterranean for several years before finally settling in central Anatolia as a permanent problem for the kings of the region.) Needing money for his new mercenaries and a new war to rebuild his prestige, Pyrrhus decided to pick on Macedon while the state was still weakened from fighting off the Galatian onslaught.

Antigonus Gonatas was unable to withstand the new assault and retreated east. By now the man who had out-survived Lysimachus, Seleucus, and Ptolemy Keraunos probably knew that all he had to do was wait out Pyrrhus as well. Sure enough, a dissident Spartan with a claim to that city's throne asked Pyrrhus to put him on it, and Pyrrhus leapt at the chance. With his enemy gone south to plunder Laconia, Gonatas gathered an army and cautiously followed.

Pyrrhus' attack on Sparta was unsuccessful. Though without city walls or an army (which was off fighting in Crete) the Spartans remained true to their warrior tradition. Old men, women and children pitched into the defence of their city. Antigonus Gonatas helped by sending a scratch squad of mercenaries as reinforcements. When the Spartan army eventually returned home at high speed the siege was lifted. Thereafter Pyrrhus was forced to retreat to the area around Argos in the eastern Peloponnese, where he was faced by the army of Gonatas, the advancing Spartans, and the people of Argos itself, who were highly suspicious of Pyrrhus' intentions.

The Argive suspicion of Pyrrhus was well-founded, for the king tried to take the city in a sneak night attack. Excellent soldier that he was, Pyrrhus managed to get into Argos without great difficulty. The problem for Pyrrhus was getting to where he wanted to be within Argos. The city was large, and Pyrrhus got lost in its winding streets. With the king not sure where he was, and the rest of Pyrrhus' army unsure what he wanted them to do, total confusion developed. Antigonus Gonatas now added to the chaos by sending his own troops into Argos.

Come dawn, and Pyrrhus was trying to evacuate his troops from the city while the rest of his army was trying to force its way in through the gates to find him. To make things even more complicated, the Epirot army had a number of elephants which could not get through the narrower gates, alleyways or arches, and thanks to the crush behind they could not turn around either. In the confusion Pyrrhus tried hard to make himself heard, and being thus conspicuous, he was an easy target. So it happened that the king of Epirus – the man who had conquered Macedonia, fought the Romans to a standstill and terrified the warriors of Sparta –was finally felled by a roof-tile to the head, flung by an anonymous old woman with a steady hand and keen eye.

Antigonus Gonatas had once again outlasted an enemy. Once they knew that Pyrrhus was dead, the leaderless Epirot army surrendered. Gonatas displayed his good sense by treating well the son of Pyrrhus when that young man was captured, and by giving Pyrrhus himself a grand funeral. Thus he made an ally of Epirus to go with the (very temporary) friendship of the Spartans and the gratitude of the Argives. To the east across the Aegean, the Seleucid king Antiochus I had his hands full with the troublesome legacy of his assassinated father, and anyway, he and Gonatas were on as friendly terms as it was possible for two Hellenistic kings to get. Ptolemy II and the Athenians were going to be a problem, but for the next five years – from 272 until 267 BC – Antigonus Gonatas had a breathing space to sort out the chaos in his kingdom and the rest of Greece.

Ptolemy II in Egypt

Ptolemy II was of a generation which never knew Alexander the Great personally but only as a venerated legend. In fact, Ptolemy was born in 308 BC, fifteen years after Alexander died in Babylon. By then his father, Ptolemy I was already ensconced in Egypt. Ptolemy II's mother, Berenice, had been married before to an obscure Macedonian nobleman. Her daughter from that marriage went on to marry Pyrrhus of Epirus.

This Berenice was the second wife of Ptolemy, who in traditional Macedonian fashion had not bothered to divorce wife number 1 (Eurydice, daughter of Antipater) before remarrying. Also in traditional Macedonian fashion, Berenice had no sooner given birth (on the Greek island of Kos, as it happened, rather than in Egypt), than she began to intrigue to have her son replace the son of Eurydice as Ptolemy

I Soter's heir. The son of Eurydice was Ptolemy Keraunos, and as we know, Berenice was successful in her scheming and Ptolemy Keraunos was exiled. Eurydice fled to the island of Miletus at the same time, thus conceding to Berenice the position of royal consort.

(This Berenice was to become considerably more famous than most Ptolemaic queens, because Ptolemy was so smitten with her that he gave her name to a seaport which he was developing on the Red Sea coast. This port lay at the end of a major road from the Egyptian interior, but its main importance lay in the fact that it was to become a major emporium for the trade with India which Berenice's son Ptolemy II was instrumental in developing.)

Under the capable guidance of his mother, Ptolemy II successfully navigated the tricky waters of a palace childhood. As a 23-year-old adult he took his first wife in a diplomatic marriage. This was Arsinoe, the daughter of Lysimachus of Thrace. This wife is commonly called Arsinoe I to distinguish her from that other Arsinoe who was his elder sister, the widow of both Lysimachus and Ptolemy Keraunos. Soon after marriage Arsinoe I delivered an heir to the royal line. The infant was naturally called Ptolemy, and in later years went on to become to become Ptolemy III.

The original Ptolemy, Ptolemy I Soter, was now a grandfather. This meant that three generations of the royal dynasty were now neatly in line for the throne as Ptolemy I, Ptolemy II and Ptolemy III. To ensure as easy a succession as possible, Ptolemy I Soter took his son on as apprentice king. Things went so smoothly that when the first Ptolemy died all that we know is that it was either late 283 or early 282 BC, and by then Ptolemy II was already in power and running the country. (The other thing we know of the death of Ptolemy I Soter is that, of all of Alexander's generals, Ptolemy I shared only with Antipater of Macedon the distinction of dying peacefully of old age, in bed with his boots off.)

Ptolemy I Soter and Seleucus had been former colleagues and then allies against Antigonus Monophthalmus. As a result relationships between the two had been peaceful, though Seleucus always resented Ptolemy's land grab of southern Syria while he was busy elsewhere. The children of these two Diadochi lacked their fathers' amity. Antiochus of Seleucia and Ptolemy II got their royal relationship off to a bad start when Ptolemy II recognized his step-brother, Ptolemy Keraunos, as king of Macedon. Antiochus claimed Macedon for himself as the heir of Seleucus, and resented Ptolemy's recognizing a rival as king – especially when that rival was the murderer of his father.

Therefore it was not long before the two Hellenistic kingdoms embarked on a brisk trial of strength. This was the so-called Carian (or Damascene) War, and it constitutes the warm-up round for a series of wars between the Ptolemies and Seleucids which are known today as the Syrian Wars.

(In the end there were six of these wars – or by some counts, seven. Since the Ptolemies proved unable to project their power beyond Egypt for long periods, and the Seleucids were unable to assail Egypt itself, the main effect of this century of warfare was to make life hellish for the people in the main combat areas. The main area in dispute was that part of southern Syria called 'Coele Syria' or 'empty Syria'. If it was not empty before hostilities began, it certainly was by the time the Hellenistic armies had repeatedly pillaged and fought their way across the landscape.)

However, the first clash of the two Hellenistic kings happened far from southern Syria, in Caria, a mountainous area in western Anatolia. While Caria's native people had an ancient culture of their own, the interest of the Hellenic kings was mainly in the Greek cities which had long been established in the area. The largest of these cities was the port of Halicarnassus, famous today as the birthplace of the historian Herodotus, and the site of one of the Seven Wonders of the ancient world – the Mausoleum. That the person buried in the Mausoleum had the name of Mausolus is not coincidental. His burial place – a tomb of epic size and splendour – was named after him, and thus it is from Mausolus that all the mausoleums in the world derive their name.

In the run-up to war, Ptolemy II had been inclined to interfere in Caria out of pure opportunism. The Egyptian fleet was the most powerful naval force in the eastern Mediterranean, just as the Carthaginian fleet was dominant in the west. (The two naval powers stayed carefully out of each other's way.) Because Caria was separated from the remainder of the Seleucid domains by at least two difficult mountain ranges, it was much easier to get to the region by sea – and Ptolemy II controlled the sea.

Antiochus retaliated for this interference by marrying one of his daughters to the ruler of Cyrenaica, a relative of Ptolemy's called Magas. Cyrenaica had been relegated to the status of a satellite state of Egypt by Ptolemy I Soter, so the diplomatic attempt to detach the area from Egyptian control was a deliberate provocation. This was all the more so as Ptolemy II noted with disquiet that Antiochus and Antigonus Gonatas of Macedon were on good terms. Therefore Ptolemy II was already feeling somewhat isolated even before Antiochus' attempts to make him even more so. Tensions rapidly flared into a full-blown war.

Exactly what happened in this round of conflict is hard to establish. Our sources are vague and murky, and much of what we know comes from the coins of regional mints. For example we know that coins from Halicarnassus had declared loyalty to Egypt by 279 BC, and that Miletus in Caria followed the change of ruler soon thereafter. We cannot now tell how much of these gains were due to successful military action and how much to political subversion. Given the later preference of Ptolemy II for diplomacy and proxy wars, one is inclined to suspect the latter. In the end both sides settled down to a wary peace after twelve months of fighting. (cf. 'The First Syrian War' W. W. Tarn, *The Journal of Hellenic Studies* Vol. 46, Part 2 (1926), pp. 155–162.)

At around this time, the Egyptian royal court acquired – or rather re-acquired – another family member. This was Arsinoe, the elder sister of Ptolemy II. She had fled Macedon after the break-up of her unhappy marriage to Ptolemy Keraunos and had been holed up on the island of Samothrace before eventually making her way to Egypt. As might be expected, Ptolemy's wife, Arsinoe I, took an immediate dislike to the arrival of this second Arsinoe and an intra-palace rivalry erupted behind the scenes.

The recently-arrived Arsinoe had more experience at scheming after her experiences at the royal courts of Lysimachus and Ptolemy Keraunos. Consequently this Arsinoe quickly identified her brother's and her rival's strengths and weaknesses. As soon as Ptolemy II had come to power he had quickly eliminated any rivals with a claim to his throne. This internal insecurity was combined with a sense of diplomatic isolation abroad. Therefore Arsinoe suggested to her brother that Arsinoe I was conspiring with Magas of Cyrenaica to assassinate him, thus neatly combining

Ptolemy II's fears of a palace coup and an external threat. It is also worth noting that with her father Lysimachus dead and his kingdom dissolved, Arsinoe I now had little political value to her husband.

Arsinoe I could play one strong card of her own, namely that she was the mother of Ptolemy's only son and presumptive heir. To counter this claim, the rival Arsinoe suggested to her brother that she should adopt the children of Arsinoe I, and thus maintain the line of royal succession without the mother. Ptolemy II considered this idea and decided that it worked for him. Accordingly he exiled Arsinoe I to a remote town in southern Egypt and thereafter married his sister, who has since become known to history as Arsinoe II. In the process Ptolemy also acquired the sobriquet by which history distinguishes him from the host of other Hellenistic Ptolemies. He is Ptolemy II Philadelphus, or 'loving of his sibling'.

While brother-sister marriage may have been practised by previous Egyptian dynasties (the matter is controversial), it was certainly a startling innovation to the Macedonians. They were accustomed to close family unions, but none *that* close. The poet Sotades unwisely commented on the pairing in satirical terms and was promptly exiled (and later killed) as a demonstration of the limits of the royal sense of humour. Another poet, Theocritus, took the wiser step of comparing the royal marriage with that of Zeus and Hera, who were also brother and sister. The arrangement was sold to the Egyptian people as being comparable to the brother-sister marriage of the Egyptian gods Osiris and Isis.

As it happened, Berenice, the mother of Ptolemy II, had died at around this time, leaving a space in Ptolemy's life for a strong female figure to guide him. Arsinoe II took adeptly to the role, to the extent where many historians consider her henceforth as pretty much co-ruler of Egypt. (There are signs that Arsinoe I was also able to make the best of her new arrangement. As the pharaoh's ex-wife she had considerable prestige, and her exile established a royal presence in a part of Egypt that had long resented that their rulers lived almost exclusively in the north. Ptolemy II gave his former spouse a generous allowance, and as far as can now be discerned Arsinoe I spent the final two decades of her life in comfortable isolation.)

This clearing of the decks on the domestic front allowed Ptolemy II to re-focus on matters abroad. As will be seen in the final part of this chapter, Antiochus of Seleucia was still struggling, partly with internal dissent, and even more with the Galatians. These had now settled in the highlands of central Anatolia and become a public menace to the surrounding states. Deciding that it was best to strike while his opponent was distracted, Ptolemy launched a swift attack that seized Damascus and the Marsayas Valley to the north.

Unfortunately for the Egyptians, Antiochus proved more capable than expected. He defeated the Gauls more swiftly than Arsinoe II had planned (as co-ruler, Arsinoe got quickly down to the business of running the war). Thereafter, Antiochus used his army to harass the Egyptian possessions in Caria and simultaneously used his diplomatic skills to stir up a revolt of Ptolemy's Gallic mercenaries in Egypt while simultaneously urging his relative by marriage, Magas of Cyrenaica, to advance on Egypt from the west. While his enemies were distracted on multiple fronts Antiochus regained control of Damascus.

Arsinoe II now put her own diplomatic skills to good use and decided that what Magas could do, she could also. Magas had advanced perilously close to Alexandria when he discovered that the Egyptians had pointed out to the Libyans that Cyrenaica was currently lacking an army. Furthermore, the Ptolemaic kingdom was prepared to sponsor an invasion of the almost defenceless territory. Magas had no choice but to precipitously abandon his invasion and hurry back to secure the home front. This left Ptolemy free to vindictively hunt down and slaughter his treacherous Gallic mercenaries.

Further north in the Aegean, the land-based army of Antiochus struggled with the difficult Anatolian terrain while the forces of Ptolemy could operate freely, thanks to their superior navy allowing transport by sea. Soon the Egyptians controlled much of the coast of southern Anatolia and Antiochus was forced to sue for peace. This, the First Syrian War, came to an end after almost four years of fighting (early 275 to late 272 BC), with the combatants agreeing to each hold on to their gains. Antiochus kept Damascus, but Ptolemy II had made major gains elsewhere in Syria and Caria. No-one doubted that the Seleucids intended the peace only as a holding action while they got their house in order. The Ptolemies were happy to go along with that. Firstly, they reckoned the Seleucid Empire was far too diverse and disorderly to ever be properly in order, and secondly they had plans for Macedon and Greece that meant putting the war in Syria on hold.

Antiochus in the Seleucid Empire

Perhaps the most surprising thing about the death of Seleucus I Nicator is that it surprised anyone. After all, simply by being a Macedonian king Seleucus already had a high-risk lifestyle. He compounded the risk by personal participation in battles (something both Ptolemy I and Ptolemy II eschewed) and in any case his age of threescore years and seventeen took him well beyond the usual lifespan of his contemporaries. Yet by all appearances his son Antiochus was taken by surprise when his father was killed.

Partly this was a political manoeuvre. Any royal heir who seemed to be planning the succession in too much detail put himself at risk, since scheduling the actual death of the current incumbent was the logical next step. Therefore to avoid execution, a wise heir would act as if the current king was going to live forever. Nevertheless, the fact that Seleucus was killed in Europe while his heir was administering the Eastern empire from Babylon left a large gap in the middle of the empire.

Almost as soon as word of the assassination of Seleucus reached the east, a rash of rebellions broke out. Exactly what happened in Syria is unclear, as all we have on record is that Antiochus chose to deal with the rebels there first, and that he did so successfully. The fact that this rebellion was both brief and contained, and caused no great damage to Syrian cities has led to the convincing suggestion that the revolt was mainly by rural native peoples dissatisfied with Hellenistic rule of any kind. (cf. Grainger, *The Rise of the Seleukid Empire*, pp 128–9).

Once he had Syria back under control, Antiochus had to tackle the far less straightforward matter of Anatolia. On a modern map, Anatolia is basically Turkey and it appears as a single unified block. Anyone fully familiar with modern Turkey will assure you that this is not actually the case, and it was far less the case in the Hellenistic era.

For a start, the region is geographically diverse with a series of mountain ranges breaking the country into a number of isolated enclaves. The largest of these mountain ranges practically wall Anatolia off from the east and southeast, while the rest of Anatolia is surrounded by sea.

In the southeast, at the elbow where the coastline of the Mediterranean turns west, we have Cilicia, sitting at the headwaters of the River Euphrates. Along the coast west of that – and comprehensively separated from Cilicia by the Taurus Mountains – are Pamphylia, Lycia and Caria. Lydia, Phrygia and Cappadocia respectively run from west to east inland to the north. To the north again, running respectively west to east along the Black Sea coast, are four other regions which we will refer to somewhat anachronistically as Pergamon, Bithynia, Paphlagonia and Pontus.

This description is an extreme simplification of the actual situation, as each region was divided into dozens of mini-states, each with a varying degree of autonomy and rulers eager to grab more if the central authority showed signs of weakening. Some of these 'states' were little more than individual castles or fortified cities with a bloody-minded attitude to cooperation, while others were minor but functional kingdoms. Note, incidentally that in the coastal regions these 'fortified cities' were more likely than not to be Greek, and the city militias were usually composed of experienced soldiers who fought in the Hellenistic style.

Because each castle and city was extremely defensible thanks to Anatolia's broken geography, conquering and administering the region had been a work in progress for Seleucus at the time of his assassination. Thereafter, the assassin Ptolemy Keraunos did his best to stir up the already volatile situation by claiming kingship over some parts of Anatolia and suggesting that he would support bids for independence of other parts.

While unstable, Anatolia remained relatively calm for several years after the death of Seleucus. This was mainly because the Hellenistic kings were desperately busy elsewhere. Things changed in 278 BC when two major players simultaneously entered the region. The first was the Seleucid army. Antigonus had regained control of the situation in Syria, and he had now come to restore his father's hegemony over Anatolia. The second arrival was the Galatian horde. This horde was a large portion of that same barbarian tidal wave that had earlier swamped Macedonia, killed Ptolemy Keraunos and devastated Delphi. Now the Galatians were in Anatolia, following a particularly bone-headed request by Nicomedes I of Bithynia who thought they might be helpful in his personal dynastic struggles.

After putting Nicomedes on the throne, the Galatians moved through Asia Minor like a wrecking ball. Some cities were sacked, some paid extortion money to save the Galatians the effort of sacking them, and others fought off the invaders. In the countryside, Galatian raiding bands wreaked havoc upon the farmers and the regional economy. It fell to Antiochus to break up the party.

Exactly what happened is uncertain, as also is when and where it happened. What we do know is that in 275 BC separate Galatian raiding bands came together and formed a major army to block the attempt of Antiochus to restore order. What the Galatians had not expected was that Antiochus had brought with him from the East a substantial number of war elephants. These huge beasts came as a shock to the barbarians, and even more of a shock to their cavalry, whose horses refused to go anywhere near them. Before the Galatians could work out a revised plan of battle, the elephants charged, accompanied by the rest of the Seleucid army.

The result was a Seleucid victory known today as 'the Elephant Battle'. Antiochus used the victory as propaganda to justify his claim to rule Asia Minor, and thereafter he referred to himself as Antiochus Soter – 'the Saviour'. Historians have been happy to go along with the name, since as with the name of Ptolemy, Seleucus and others, a host of other Antiochi were to follow in the footsteps of this first king. Therefore the name 'Soter' has stuck even though the 'elephant victory' was less comprehensive than Antiochus claimed. Far from being extirpated, the Galatians were able to retreat to the Anatolian interior, and there set up a kingdom which outlasted that of their Hellenic opponents. (cf Altay Coşkun, 'Deconstructing a Myth Of Seleucid History: The So-Called "Elephant Victory" Revisited', *Phoenix* 66, no. 1/2 (2012): 57–73.)

The defeat of the Galatians might have been more comprehensive had Antiochus been able to follow up his victory and crush the Galatians while they were still reeling from defeat. This opportunity was denied to Antiochus by the husband and wife team of Ptolemy II and Arsinoe II who decided that while Antiochus and his army were entangled in Asia Minor they would take the chance to make further gains in Syria. The result was the First Syrian War which has already been described (p.96). At the end of this war, Antiochus accepted that the Ptolemies had got the upper hand, and he temporarily conceded the fact in a peace treaty which confirmed the Ptolemaic gains.

In part, this concession was because Antiochus had work to do in the east. Like most of his successors, Antiochus had to spent much of his time in Syria, because that was the interface between the Seleucid kingdom and the other Hellenistic states. Nevertheless, the Seleucid domains stretched thousands of kilometres to the east. Administering these eastern domains while simultaneously dealing with crisis after crisis in the west was to prove an impossible challenge, and this was the main reason why the East slowly slipped out of the Seleucid grasp. When war broke out with Ptolemy in 275 BC, Antiochus sent his son Seleucus to Babylon to act as his regent there. By the end of the war it was clear that this son had become dangerously independence-minded and there was a risk that he might form a breakaway kingdom of his own.

Antiochus was unable to get away until 269 BC, when he took himself and a substantial army east and in due course he dealt with the independence movement by killing off his son and temporarily taking the reins himself. It will be remembered that Antiochus had personal connections with the East. His mother was from Sogdiana, and Antiochus had earlier in his career administered the East for his father Seleucus I Nicator. During this first spell as administrator in the East, Antiochus had been successful in fighting off incursions by large tribes of barbarian nomads, so the return of the king was a generally welcome event. While in Babylonia, Antiochus further endeared himself to the locals by rebuilding the Ezida temple.

At this time news would have reached him that the Ptolemies were entangled in Greece, fighting a proxy war (the Chremonidian War) with Antigonus Gonatas. This meant that for a few years Antiochus had some breathing space to sort out his disorganized kingdom.

The Chremonidian War

Chremonides was an Athenian stoic philosopher. As was often the case with the energetic and ambitious Athenians, Chremonides had also diversified in other directions, in this case geopolitics and local politics. In local politics he had become leader of the Athenians. Geopolitically, Chremonides opened talks with Sparta on the topic of regaining the domination of Greece that the two states had enjoyed during the Classical era.

One might expect that the Spartans would be reluctant to get involved, since the plans of Chremonides involved throwing off the Macedonian hegemony of Antigonus Gonatas and making Greece 'independent'. It will be remembered that Sparta owed Antigonus a considerable debt for saving the city from the predations of Pyrrhus. However, the Spartans were notoriously stingy with their gratitude, and they had their own agenda. On this the first item was regaining control of Messenia. For over 300 years of the Classical era, Sparta had dominated its richer and more populous neighbour to the east and that domination had made Sparta the foremost city in Greece. Sparta desperately wanted Messenia back, and knew this was not going to happen while Antigonus Gonatas was calling the shots in southern Greece.

All parties knew that fighting the well-equipped veteran Macedonian army was going to require money and mercenaries. Fortunately they had assurances that these would be forthcoming, along with supplies of grain and war materiel, for the would-be rebels had found a powerful patron in Ptolemy II.

We can be almost certain that Ptolemy's interest in the freedom of Greece started with his deep dislike of Antigonus Gonatas and stopped well short of any ideological attachment to the independence movement. More particularly, Ptolemy was annoyed by the fact that Antigonus had been building a fleet to challenge Egyptian naval dominance of the Aegean. Ptolemy felt that a diversion in southern Greece would both divert the energies of his rival and also hopefully present the occasion for a naval engagement in which Antigonus' fledgling fleet could be crushed before it got any stronger.

Once Athens and Sparta had the required assurances of help from Ptolemy the two cities declared their independence in 267 BC and waited for Antigonus to react. This reaction was slow in coming. The cautious Antigonus was not going to be rushed into anything. He wanted to prepare his army, and even more, he wanted to prepare his fleet.

Antigonus Gonatas took some minor hits during the first two years of the war, though no serious fighting took place. Then, when he was ready, Antigonus marched slowly south bringing Greek city-states back under his control as he did so. The Spartans decided to make a stand at the Isthmus of Corinth. Under their king Areus I the Spartans fought a spirited battle. However, the era of the city-state was done. The days when a city's army of some 6,000 mostly part-time soldiers could have a major influence on events had ended with the Persian Wars. In contemporary Greece, an army of around 20,000 mostly professional soldiers appears to have been optimal. An army that size needed a nation-state to raise and support it, and an army of 20,000 is exactly what the nation-state of Macedon brought to the battle.

(More than 20,000 soldiers presented an army quartermaster with a logistical nightmare. Greece was poor and mountainous and even an army of 20,000 had to keep moving if it intended to live off the land. This left local farmers very little to live on after so large an army had passed by, which is another reason why Greece was relatively depopulated by the Roman era.)

The Spartan army was crushed, and the Spartan king killed. For Sparta, this battle represented one of the last attempts by a city in decline to again become relevant in Greek affairs. Thereafter Sparta effectively became a small, and highly recalcitrant mountain state, too wracked by internal discord to matter in the larger political scene.

Bereft of their Spartan allies, the Athenians retreated behind their walls and waited confidently for Ptolemy's fleet to keep them supplied. Disillusion and hunger grew steadily in Athens as the months went by and Ptolemy did nothing to supply the aid which he had promised. It may have been that Ptolemy's logistical situation was simply too chaotic to get a relief force to Athens in time. It is more probable that, with Sparta taken out of the picture, Ptolemy correctly reckoned that Athens was incapable of withstanding Antigonus alone.

Therefore, any support given to Athens would only prolong the time until that city's inevitable defeat and all that time there would be considerable cost and embarrassment to Egypt. The Hellenistic kings never flinched from brutal realpolitik, and if it seemed to Ptolemy that Athens was no longer useful, then he would abandon the city without a second thought. The problem was one of perception – if Ptolemy did not even make a pretence of helping the Athenians, then he would totally lack credibility when he attempted to incite trouble through proxies elsewhere. Therefore he did get a relief effort under way, but too late. It is probable that famine had forced the Athenians to surrender long before the Egyptian fleet had left the harbour.

In any case, the relief effort never reached Athens, for Antigonus had not given up working on his war fleet. Fully equipped and trained, this fleet met the Egyptian reinforcements off the island of Cos (exactly when in uncertain) and soundly defeated it.

Chapter 7

The West

The Macedon of Antigonus Gonatas

For two generations, from Alexander's accession to the throne in 336 BC to the end of the Chremonidian War in 260 BC, the Greek world had been in turmoil. War had been endemic in Greece long before the time of Alexander, but consequent territorial changes had been few. This changed dramatically when, after brutally re-establishing the Macedonian hegemony after his father's death, Alexander led the Greeks on his heady adventure of conquest and exploration in the East.

The eastern limits of the Greek world, which had once stopped at the shores of the Black Sea, now touched the western states of India. From being remote and fabled, Babylon was now one of the core cities of the Seleucid Empire. Nor was this expansion merely territorial. As well as soldiers and settlers, Greek scholars had flocked to the new lands in the East. The expansion of the Greek world was as much intellectual as it was physical. While geographers, naturally, had a field day, there was also – for example – plenty for mathematicians and astronomers to explore in the records of the Babylonians.

Even before the Babylonians, the Sumerians had set a basic standard by dividing a circle into six equal segments. Regarding the heavens as a huge circle, the Babylonian quest for astronomical precision had divided each of these sections into another sixty parts, thus passing on to the Greeks and the modern world the current division of a circle into 360 degrees. Since no-one had managed to measure seconds precisely, it was felt that 60 minutes was enough for the standard astronomical hour. Later, the same division was made for seconds, which is why we have 3,600 seconds in an hour.

While astronomers were exploring the heavens, naturalists were examining the huge variety of previously almost-legendary creatures which were now present and very real. The crocodile and rhinoceros were available for study and dissection, while hope of finding dragons and griffons was fading fast. There were also new foods to try and, after exposure to Zoroastrianism and Indian philosophy, new ideas to discuss.

In short, the turmoil following the conquests of Alexander was by no means only military and political. The Greek world had blossomed into an almost limitless expanse of possibilities. Any stark study of the political struggles of the Hellenistic kings fails to take into account the underlying wonder and romance that the era had for the Greeks. There were castles and kings, hidden cities with strange religions, elephants and pirates. There were a host of states and cities each with their own set of palace intrigues, from disputes over a petty chieftainship somewhere in the Armenian highlands to backstabbing queens and princesses in the royal courts.

Far from a forgotten appendix of history to be squeezed between the classical and Roman eras, the Hellenistic age was an age of humanism, intellectual and scientific development, played out across a colourful and diverse backdrop. It is to the individual parts of that backdrop we now turn.

Macedon and the Persian menace

During the era of Persian expansion (560–490 BC), Macedon had been constantly threatened by its huge neighbour to the east. This threat became reality in the late sixth century when the Persians crossed into Europe and set about subduing the restive tribes to the north of the Greek peninsula. In one way this Persian invasion was helpful to the Macedonians, for the defeat of the barbarians eased the military pressure and gave them breathing space to properly organize themselves as a state. The Macedonian king at the time was Amyntas I, and some historians recognize him as the first king of Macedon proper.

Amyntas may have been king, but an absolute ruler he was not. The Persian armies demanded that he hand over the symbolic gifts of earth and water as a token of Macedonian submission to Persia. In other words, Macedon started out as a Persian vassal state. This was something the southern Greeks later used as a constant reproach to the Macedonians, criticizing what they (unfairly) saw as craven Macedonian surrender and comparing it with their own heroic fight to keep their independence.

The son of King Amyntas was called Alexander (the first – Alexander the Great was Alexander the third). Under Alexander I the slow growth of Persian power in the Balkan region saw Macedon become completely absorbed into the Persian polity as part of a larger western satrapy, an area which included Thrace and some formerly independent cities along the coast.

'The Macedonians were added to the number of the slaves of the [Persian] king' says the historian Herodotus bluntly (*The History*, book 5) – which is a bit rich coming from the historian whose home town of Halicarnassus had been under Persian rule for generations. Nevertheless, the fact remained that, like the Greek cities of Asia Minor, Macedon knew Persian domination. Much to later Macedonian embarrassment, Macedonian soldiers fought alongside their Persian counterparts at the epic battles of Thermopylae and Plataea. In fact, King Alexander of Macedon accompanied the Persian King Xerxes on that invasion of Greece, and Alexander was involved in negotiations with the Greeks after the Battle of Salamis in 480 BC.

The Persian defeat at Plataea in 479 BC marked the high point of Persian expansion into Europe. The Persian land army which was destroyed in that battle was the last serious Persian military presence in Greece. Even before then, Herodotus informs us, Alexander was unhappy with Persian domination and did what he could to help the Greeks. He declared Macedon independent the moment the last Persian soldier left his territory. But thereafter, even as Macedon grew as a kingdom and developed a formidable army under Archelaus I (413–399 BC), the threat of a Persian reoccupation never went away.

This was the background against which Philip II, the father of Alexander the Great came to power. Philip, like his ancestor Alexander I, was of the Argead dynasty, a family that traced its ancestry back to Argos in the heroic age of almost a thousand years previously. It was Philip who sensed that the Persian behemoth was in decline and vulnerable to invasion by the numerically vastly inferior Greeks.

It was also Philip who, by a combination of brute force and persuasive diplomacy persuaded the southern Greeks to recognize Macedon as a

Hellenic state. Before Philip the Argead kings had been recognized as Greeks because of their reputed ancestry, but their subjects were – in Greek eyes – barbarians. Modern historians consider this a bit harsh, pointing out that in both language and culture the Macedonians and southern Greeks had more things in common than differences.

Nevertheless, it is only after Macedon was formally admitted to membership of the sacred Amphictyonic League in 346 BC that we can officially refer to the Macedonians as 'Greeks'. This is because only Greek peoples could be members of the League, so by admitting the Macedonians to the League the Greeks were formally recognizing the Macedonians' 'Greek' status (or conferring it, depending on one's point of view). In any case it was certainly as Greeks that the Macedonians of Alexander the Great headed the Hellenic League in its conquest of the East – a conquest which forever lifted the threat of a Persian invasion from Macedonian minds.

Sadly, in terms of achieving its strategic intention the Macedonian invasion of Persia was nevertheless a failure. The idea was to make sure that the eastern empire could no longer threaten Macedon. Now the Persians were gone, but after Alexander the threat of invasion from the east became more rather than less acute. The 'eastern empire' remained. It was now Seleucid rather than Persian, but it was every bit as hostile.

It actually made things worse for Antigonus Gonatas and his successors that the potential invaders were fellow Macedonians: the rulers of the Seleucid and Ptolemaic kingdoms. As we have seen, a side effect of the wars of the Diadochi was the virtual extinction of the ancient Argead line. However, before that extinction took place most of Alexander's generals had managed to link themselves to the Argeads through strategic marriages to various royal daughters. Now both the Ptolemies and Seleucids had at least as strong a claim to the Macedonian throne as did Antigonus.

Therefore, throughout the Hellenistic era Macedon faced the same strategic threats as it had throughout the preceding Classical era. That is, the threats of invasion from powerful neighbours to the east and barbarian states in the north and west. The major difference was that the Macedonians now had control of Greece to the south. They were to spend the Hellenistic era trying desperately to maintain that hegemony.

Geography

If ancient etymology is to be believed, the name of 'Macedonian' can be roughly translated as 'highlander'. If so, the name is appropriate as mountains played a large part in shaping the Macedonian kingdom. The original Macedonians probably started in the far south of their later kingdom as farmers on the plains of the River Haliacmon which runs eastward along the northern foothills of the Olympus range.

The Olympus range, with its forbidding mountains and steep, easily-defended passes meant that Macedon was generally secure from attack from the south. With that flank secure, the Macedonians gradually pushed north and east, absorbing or displacing Thracian tribes along the way. Eventually they reached another defensible mountain range, this being where the Rhodope Mountains run south-eastwards to the Aegean sea. In later years the Macedonians were to push further east, so that Philip II founded the eponymous town of Philippolis on the River Hebron (now Plovdiv in modern Bulgaria). However, the new conquests never became a part of the core kingdom as did the lands west of the Rhodope range.

Here, under the capable generalship of Alexander I, the Macedonians took on the tribes of the Paeonians, Pelagonians and others as they pushed northwest. Eventually the northern border came to rest against yet another mountain range: the Scardus Mountains. The far western border was never fully secured thanks to the territorial ambitions of the warlike Illyrians and Dardanians. After Alexander, the Epirots to the southwest also tried to establish a presence in the area.

Nevertheless, untidy western border aside, Macedonia came into the Hellenistic era as a compact and highly defensible kingdom. Macedonia was also distinct in being an integrated nation-state. That is, the rulers of Macedon were Macedonians and they ruled a people who identified as Macedonians and shared a common language, culture and religion.

Compare this with the Ptolemies: Macedonians who now identified themselves firmly with the culture of southern Greece, and who ruled the still largely separate kingdoms of Upper and Lower Egypt from a Hellenistic capital which was quickly gaining a large Jewish population in addition to the existing mix of Greeks and Egyptians. Or the Seleucids, who ruled an untidy mess of animists, Zoroastrians, Jews and worshippers of the ancient Gods of Babylonia as overlords of dozens of kingdoms which were run by everything from Greek democrats to hereditary priestly castes.

That was the good news. The bad news was that the main reason why the Macedonians had an efficient integrated kingdom was because they needed to have one in order to survive. Macedon never had the wealth of the Seleucid or Egyptian kingdoms, and the state lacked even the population of the wild barbarian lands to the north. This meant that even at the height of Macedonian power the threat of barbarian invasion never went away.

Any time that the Macedonian army was engaged elsewhere, be it in Thrace or southern Greece, the barbarian tribes came together to plan what were essentially huge pillaging raids. This severely limited the ability of Macedonian kings to do much outside their own domains, and even military adventures in Greece were conducted with the Macedonian generals keeping an anxious watch over their shoulders for messengers bearing bad news from the north.

Southern Greece

The Greece of the Classical era left behind a pale shadow of itself in the Hellenistic era. The Greek peninsula lacks the ability to produce any crop more substantial than its mountains, which by most counts take up some eighty per cent of the landscape. There are few substantial rivers in southern Greece, fewer lakes, and very limited amounts of arable land.

Unsurprisingly, there were considerable and very lively debates as to who owned that arable land, with the result that warfare was endemic in Greece until the Roman era. Equally unsurprisingly, the Greeks from earliest times showed a strong readiness to abandon their homeland and settle elsewhere, since the grass was literally greener almost anywhere else. As a result, by the classical era the southern Greeks had established cities in Iberia, Africa and the Crimea. Almost always these were on the coast ('squatting around the Mediterranean like frogs around a pond', as Socrates is said to have remarked in Plato's *Phaedo* 109b).

In the Hellenistic era the people of southern Greece eagerly heeded the siren call of the Seleucid and Ptolemaic kings, abandoned their stony fields and flocked to settle in the new cities founded on fertile fields alongside the Euphrates, the Nile and the Orontes. With the farmers went soldiers, farriers, merchants and their families, until Greece itself was mostly left with those either too poor to emigrate, or too rich to want to.

Peace did not follow depopulation. There might have been more land to go around, but hundreds of years of intercity combat had ingrained warfare into the social psyche of the *polis* culture. To make a somewhat ambitious generalization, the concept of 'peace' to a contemporary Greek meant a period when one did not currently have an enemy to fight. Likewise, one made peace with another city-state in order to make available resources needed to fight someone else.

Spartan society was notoriously built on the basis of producing and supporting a warrior caste, yet Sparta only produced in an exaggerated form what all other Greek states did also. For example, in Athens a young male citizen was enrolled as an *ephebe* soon after adolescence. Ephebes were taught civic responsibilities, but above all they were taught to be soldiers. Thereafter, until the age of sixty men were expected to provide (unpaid) military service to the state during a campaigning season that lasted from the time after the sowing of crops until the harvest.

The quality of a Greek's armour and weapons (his panoply) determined his social status, and a good panoply was a treasured family possession. So much did the Greeks take warfare for granted that – for example – most biographies of Socrates do not mention that he was also a ferocious fighter. Those that do mention this fact do so mainly because it was on the battlefield that Socrates once saved the life of the notorious politician Alcibiades. (It later turned out it would have been much better if he had not bothered.)

In the Hellenistic era warfare changed in type but not in intensity. The departure of peasant farmers for the East meant that vacant land fell into the hands of those rich enough to buy it up, rather than into the hands of the poor who actually needed it. These landless poor found ready employment as mercenaries. All of the Hellenistic kings were desperate for soldiers – to the extent that soldiers captured after a battle were usually pressed straight into the army of the victor – so many Greeks were professional soldiers. Even Sparta in this era was so short of manpower that the state generally employed as many mercenaries as it could afford.

The other change was that in the Classical era warfare was usually an unproductive affair fought between individual cities. 'Unproductive' because wars achieved very little. The political mechanisms of the *polis* combined with the rugged landscape of Greece to make ruling another city almost impossible, and the limited number of city sites meant that on the rare occasions when a city was demolished, a new one would promptly arise on the ruins. Thus, even after total defeat in the Peloponnesian War of 431–404 BC, Athens had regained its independence and strength within a generation.

In the Hellenistic era, Macedonian armies kept the aspirations of individual Greek cities in check by their sheer size. In the Classical era, an army of 6,000 men was a force to be reckoned with. In the Hellenistic era 20,000 men were needed to make the same impression, and few city-states could come up with that sort of manpower. Therefore cities seldom fought alone. Sometimes the alliances were temporary, such as the combination of Athens and Sparta against Macedon in the Chremonidian War. Other leagues were more permanent, such as the Achaean League. This league was formed in 281 BC and was to grow steadily over the following decades to become a major headache for the Macedonian kings.

The Achaean League might have drawn its inspiration from the even older Aetolian League which dominated western Greece north of the Peloponnese. The League had long existed as a loose confederation, but was at this time tightening its political structures and had recently taken control of the sacred site of Delphi. The Aetolians had been one of the few Greek states to successfully fight off the Galatian invasion of 280 BC, and this added considerably to their prestige.

The Aetolian and Achaean leagues were contiguous and given the nature of Greek society as described above, it should come as no surprise that the pair fought like cats in a sack. This hostility was strongly encouraged by the Antigonid kings of Macedon, on the basis that the Aetolians had rebelled in the 320s BC and Macedon had never really succeeded in bringing them to heel thereafter. Therefore, from the Macedonian point of view, the more the Achaeans could hurt the Aetolians the better, and since the Achaeans were probably going to fight somebody anyway, the Aetolians were an excellent choice.

Of the other formerly-great Greek states, Thebes had never recovered from the drastic after-effects of its rebellions against the Macedonian kings. After Alexander pillaged and demolished Thebes, Cassander had paid for the rebuilding of the city and its walls. These walls lasted only until the city was captured by Demetrios, the son of Antigonus Monophthalmus in 292 BC. Classical Thebes had drawn much of its strength from its control of the rest of Boeotia, but now, with that area largely under the control of the Aetolian League, Thebes itself was politically insignificant.

In much the same way, Sparta was never the same once it had been stripped of its possession of the neighbouring state of Messenia at the end of the Classical era. Short of money and manpower, the Spartan kings were as obsessed with regaining control of Messenia as the Achaean League was determined to stop them. This preoccupation and lack of strategic reach meant that Sparta was in our period (as one historian puts it) 'a Peloponnesian squabbler' of little interest to anyone but historians and the city's immediate neighbours.

Athens also was not the city it had once been, but it was closer. The location on the south coast of Attica made the Athenian port of the Piraeus a trading nexus, and skilful diplomacy combined with a useful fleet made the Athenians a force to be reckoned with in the Aegean. As a result, the Athenians were courted by the Ptolemies. Even the disappointing lack of support from Ptolemy II in the Chremonidian War was not enough to fully disillusion the Athenians. Egyptian-Athenian relations remained close and were yet another of the many irritations which the Macedonian overlords of southern Greece had to cope with.

Overall, how far Greece had fallen, and how far it was yet to fall can be seen in a letter written by the Roman Servius Sulpicius in the first century BC.

On my journey from Asia [Minor], *I was sailing from Aegina towards Megara, and began to take stock of the places that were all about me. Aegina was behind me, Megara in front. On my right was the Piraeus, on my left Corinth. All of these places were once flourishing but now all that met my eyes was ruin and decay.*

(Servius Sulpicius to Cicero, *ad fam*, 27.)

By and large, much of this 'ruin and decay' had happened by 275 BC – not despite the epic Greek success in overthrowing the mighty Persian Empire, but as a direct result of having done so.

Balanced between: the precarious states of Pergamon and Bithynia

Histories of the Hellenistic kingdoms understandably focus on the Big Three of Macedon, the Seleucids and Ptolemaic Egypt. After all, these kingdoms were large, militarily and economically powerful and their stories are complex and rich enough to absorb a historian's full attention. Yet these were not the only Hellenistic kingdoms of the era.

In northwest Anatolia, at the very edge of the Seleucid Empire and just close enough to Macedon for Seleucid control to be effectively challenged, two small kingdoms managed to struggle to an insecure independence. Over the years that followed, a succession of competent kings took advantage of the difficulties and preoccupations of the Seleucids to put their edge kingdoms on a firmer foundation.

Pergamon

Some 300 miles (500 km) south of Byzantium, this Hellenistic kingdom was a small city-state of absolutely no significance in the Classical era. One of the very few references to the place in all that time is by the writer Xenophon who mentions that the epic March of the Ten Thousand (the *Anabasis*) finished at Pergamon when the Greek mercenaries whom Xenophon commanded completed their long journey from Mesopotamia to the sea.

For all its obscurity, Pergamon had a useful city site. The royal palace – which did double duty as the city's acropolis – sat at the top of a substantial hill on the northern side of the Caicus Valley. The rest of the city spread out on the slopes below. The whole city was some sixteen miles (25 km) from the sea. This distance meant that the city was far enough inland that it could not be surprised by a sudden naval assault, but close enough to keep in touch with the Mediterranean world through the port of Elaia, which served Pergamon rather as the port of Ostia served Rome.

The area was conquered – or as they would say 'liberated' – by the Greeks in the campaigns of Alexander the Great. In the subsequent wars of the Diadochi, Pergamon came under the control of Lysimachus of Thrace. The death of Lysimachus brought about the end of Thracian rule in Pergamon, and left the city in something of an administrative limbo. Macedon claimed most of European Thrace, but was in too much of a mess to effectively project power into Asia Minor. The Seleucids awarded themselves control of the city, but they were too distant to exercise full control and Antiochus I had much larger issues to deal with.

Therefore the commander whom Lysimachus had sent to administer the city ended up as its *de facto* ruler. This was a man called Philetaerus, and one of the few things we know of him was that his father was a Greek from Asia Minor who was called Attalus. For all the history of Pergamon as an independent entity, Pergamon was ruled by the descendants of this Attalus, who are usually referred to as the Attalid dynasty.

Philetaerus was to prove one of the best things that happened to Pergamon for he was both competent and long-lived. Over the next forty years until his death in 263 BC, while chaos surrounded him, Philetaerus fortified and beautified his new city while simultaneously extending its territory. Philetaerus was sterile, apparently as a result of a childhood incident, so on his death the city passed to the control of an adopted son, his former nephew Eumenes I.

Philetaerus had been happy enough to accept Seleucid rule so long as this was no more than nominal. Eumenes was more of an independent thinker, and as such declared Pergamon independent soon after he came to power. In this he was supported by Ptolemy II of Egypt. As ever, the interfering Ptolemy was happy to supply logistical support and money to anyone who had a good chance of embarrassing his rival Hellenistic rulers. It is probable that Ptolemaic money paid for mercenaries that bolstered the Pergamene army when Antiochus I came to personally restore Seleucid authority over Pergamon.

The Pergamenes were consequently able to defeat Antiochus in a battle fought in 261 BC near the former Persian regional capital of Sardis. Thereafter Antiochus accepted that the Pergamenes felt too strongly about independence for it to be worth him pressing the point. He had more important things to do than dedicate his time to subduing a small breakaway state on the periphery of his kingdom, especially as that state had never really been under Seleucid control anyway.

By way of demonstrating Pergamon's new-found sovereignty, Eumenes had the city mint produce coins which depicted not Seleucid rulers as before, but the image of Philetaerus – a coinage which became traditional in the time of his successors. Often the reverse of Pergamene coins showed Athena, the patron goddess of the city. The Goddess of Wisdom was an appropriate choice, because under the Attalids the city rapidly became a haven for scholars. The library of Pergamon in time became so famous that the Ptolemies, jealous of the reputation of the Library at Alexandria (p.146) refused to supply papyrus for the Pergamene library's scrolls.

This decision was to have far-reaching consequences. The inventive scholars at Pergamon sought other material to write upon. A substitute was readily at hand in the form of animal skin stretched extremely thin and rubbed smooth. This material had been in use previously in Asia Minor, but the Pergamenes developed it to an unprecedented degree. Indeed, so much did they popularize the use of this material that the modern name for this material – parchment – is a corruption of the word 'Pergamon'.

This is important, because centuries later, as the Roman Empire began slowly to collapse, papyrus from Egypt became unavailable. Scholars switched to using parchment, and those – precious few – who maintained libraries had works copied on to parchment as their papyrus texts crumbled with age and use. It is not too broad a generalization to say that most works transferred to parchment have survived to the modern era. Almost none of the texts left on papyrus have done so. In other words, without the contribution of Pergamon our knowledge of the world of antiquity might have been much, much poorer.

Though Pergamon had thrown off Seleucid rule and expanded its domains considerably since then, the new state's independence was severely crippled by the nearby Galatians. It is very probable that the Pergamenes under Eumenes had to pay a very substantial tribute to keep the Galatians off their necks. Given the capricious nature of these barbarian neighbours it was dubious that even the tribute could keep the state safe forever.

Bithynia

North and east of Pergamon was Bithynia. Like Pergamon, Bithynia rose from the wreckage of the Persian Empire after the conquest of Alexander. However, Alexander and his successors were too preoccupied to stamp their authority across all of the complex geopolitical puzzle which was ancient Anatolia. Consequently the Bithynians did not boldly declare their independence but instead sneaked away from the rule of Alexander and the Diadochi without anyone noticing.

While the first rulers of Pergamon were kings in all but name, the native aristocrats to whom fell the rule of Bithynia were not so shy. They took the name of 'king' from the start. Tiboetes I (326–278 BC) was the first of two long-lived monarchs who set the kingdom on a secure footing. As he tried to expand Bithynia's borders, Tiboetes clashed with Antigonus Monophthalmus and later with both Lysimachus and Antigonus Gonatas. As with Pergamon, Bithynia was saved from a major attempt at conquest by the Diadochi because of its lack of importance in the current geopolitical situation, and the ferocity with which the capable rulers of these two states defended their independence.

As the distinctly non-Greek name of Tiboetes suggests, the family which came to rule Bithynia was not Greek in origin. However, Greek cities – especially nearby Chalcedon – had culturally influenced the area for centuries. The second king of Bithynia, who came to power on the death of Tiboetes in 278 BC, had the thoroughly Greek name of Nicomedes (meaning 'victorious over the Persians').

Nicomedes was to go on to found a new capital – Nicomedia – on the site of an existing Greek city. This was Astarkus, birthplace of the historian Arrian to whom we owe much of what we know of the campaigns of Alexander. Thus Nicomedia was a Greek city from the start and it remained so as the Bithynian capital. Indeed, the city was to remain a centre of Hellenic culture in the region for the next 600 years or so.

Nicomedes maintained the independence of his kingdom by playing off the great Hellenic powers against each other. A good example of this is that just before his death in 255 BC, he made his infant son his heir and placed the child under the joint guardianship of Ptolemy II and Antigonus Gonatas.

Syracuse: a Hellenistic Kingdom in the West

The stirring events in the east of the Greek world rather tend to crowd off the stage those other Greek states which existed right across the known world to the west. Here we have the excuse that most of the western Greek settlements were not kingdoms but *poleis* – small city-states of little individual significance. Most of these consisted of a single city – the *polis* – and a hinterland – the *chora*. Apart from farming the small amount of territory in the *chora* these cities maintained their economies by trading with the native peoples for whom they often acted as a gateway to the wider Mediterranean world.

The coast of Sicily was densely settled with Greek cities which, in traditional Greek style, feuded with each other; they also fought the Carthaginians who had settled in the west of the island, and the native peoples, the Sicels, whom they had driven inland. Thus Sicily was considered a part of Magna Graecia – Greater Greece, under which name the Greeks lumped all the cities of Italy and Sicily.

The most powerful of these cities was undoubtedly Syracuse. The city was already half a millennium old by the time of Alexander. It had a considerable hinterland, and a population of somewhere around a quarter of a million inhabitants. This made Syracuse a very formidable state indeed, as the Athenians discovered when they tried to conquer Syracuse while at the height of their power in 415 BC. The attempt proved catastrophic for the Athenians, whose expeditionary force of thousands of men and hundreds of warships was almost entirely wiped out. This loss was a major factor leading to the subsequent defeat and capture of Athens by which the Spartans ended the drawn-out Peloponnesian War.

Syracuse interspersed episodes of democratic rule with the autocratic rule of tyrants. 'Tyrant' in the Greek use of the term were not necessarily tyrannical – and indeed some of the tyrants of Syracuse were highly enlightened despots. It was one of these tyrants, Dionysus II (367–344 BC, with interludes in exile), who took exception to the flattery of a courtier who repeatedly informed him that he was the happiest of men.

Dionysus invited the man to take his place at a royal banquet, and at the height of the festivities enquired of the courtier how he liked being the 'ruler' of Syracuse. On being informed that it was just great,

Dionysus drew the courtier's attention to a sword suspended by a single hair above the ruler's seat. Were that hair to snap, the sword would drop from a considerable height to end up impaling the courtier between his shoulders. That, Dionysus grimly informed the courtier, was the fate of a ruler. The taste of the good things in life was somewhat soured by the fact that it was all rather precarious. By a twist of fate the sword, which certainly belonged to Dionysus, is known to posterity as the 'Sword of Damocles' after the name of the courtier.

At the start of the Hellenistic era Syracuse came under heavy military pressure from the Carthaginians. The city appealed for help to Pyrrhus of Epirus, who arrived in 278 BC with dreams of establishing an Italian empire. Pyrrhus drove off the Carthaginians, but for a brief period the city ended up under Epirot rule. However, Pyrrhus and his army did not stay long and in 275 BC a native son called Hiero took power. Hiero was the second of that name to rule in Syracuse, but Hiero II is usually referred to as 'king' rather than 'tyrant' of Syracuse. One reason for this was that Hiero ruled for an uncommonly long time, and after his fifty-year rule the Syracusans had largely forgotten about other forms of government.

An astute politician, Hiero was quick to ally with the rising power of Rome. In this Pyrrhus had shown the way. Until the arrival of Pyrrhus in Italy, the Greeks of Sicily and elsewhere had considered the Romans as just another barbarian state enjoying a temporary spell of local dominance. Few considered the Roman legions a serious match for the skilled veteran army of Pyrrhus, and no-one – except possibly the Romans themselves – expected that the legions would be able to fight Pyrrhus to a standstill. Yet they did, and in so doing the Romans first attracted the serious attention of the Hellenistic world.

Consequently, Hiero readily accepted an alliance with Rome against the Carthaginians in the First Punic War, an epic struggle for dominance in the West which started at about the same time as Antiochus II kicked off the Second Syrian War of 260 BC against Ptolemy II in the East.

Rather as Pergamon compensated for its small size by becoming a beacon of scholarship, the rulers of Syracuse had long been known as patrons of philosophy and the arts. In 287 BC Syracuse added to its fame by becoming the birthplace of perhaps the greatest scientist in the ancient world: Archimedes.

Archimedes

One of the great strengths of Hellenism lay in the fact that science and religion did not mix. Greek religion lacked dogma – that set of beliefs laid down by church authorities as incontrovertibly true. This meant that Greek scientists and philosophers were able to follow the evidence wherever it led without ending up in painful disputes with the religious authorities. Furthermore – and unlike the later Romans – Greek rulers had the very modern attitude that successful scientists and inventors added lustre to their rule and consequently such people were encouraged.

In short, the seed that was the genius of Archimedes was raised on fertile ground. Archimedes was born some time between 295 and 285 BC. (We are told that he was 75 at the time of his death which would put his birth date at 287 BC, but the precise age was probably chosen by his biographer more for narrative convenience than accurate dating.) Archimedes was probably of aristocratic origins as it is commonly believed that his family was able to afford the cost of study in Egypt for the young prodigy. Thereafter it is believed that Archimedes did not leave his native city – which makes him one of a large number of famous 'Greeks' who never set foot in mainland Greece.

Very little else is known of the life of Archimedes apart from his mathematical discoveries and mechanical inventions, quite possibly because apart from math and inventions, Archimedes did not actually have much of a life. We are told that while working on a problem he had to be reminded to perform basic functions such as eating and sleeping.

Mathematically, Archimedes pushed the field further than any other single man until the discovery of calculus. Even there Archimedes came up with some conclusions which suggest that he was getting close. However, the great scientist would probably fail most modern secondary school maths exams because of his persistent failure to show his work. We know for example that he managed to calculate the square root of three to within four decimal points of the exact answer, but we have no idea of how he did it.

The work of which Archimedes was most proud was the set of convoluted calculations by which he was able to calculate the volume and relative mathematical relationships between a sphere and a cylinder. We know that because he asked for a sphere and cylinder to be placed on his tomb. However, the discovery for which Archimedes is most famous is that which led to the original 'eureka!' moment.

Hiero had given a goldsmith a quantity of pure gold with which to make a crown. When the completed work was returned the king developed an uneasy suspicion that the gold in the crown had been partly adulterated with silver. Since one of the useful things about having geniuses around the palace was that such problems could be referred to them, Archimedes was given the job of determining if the crown was indeed pure gold – but to do so without damaging the crown in any way. Evidently, even if he did not eat or sleep while working on a problem, the great scientist still took his baths, because he was pondering the question as he climbed into the tub.

He noted that the water was displaced by his body and realized (as one does) that if he divided the weight of the crown by the amount of water that the crown displaced by being dunked into a tub of its own, the relative density could be determined. If the relative density was less than the equivalent amount of pure gold, then the metal was indeed no longer pure. Delighted by his discovery, he bounded from tub to workshop, clad in no more than a film of rapidly drying moisture, and immediately put his theory to the test. Unfortunately for the goldsmith, he and the crown were found wanting. (While the best-known story about Archimedes, this one has a few flaws. Displacement is too inexact for the fine measurements that calculating the weight of alloys requires. More probably Archimedes employed his breakthrough in fluid mechanics which is still called the Archimedes principle today.)

A quick study of some of the other mathematical works of Archimedes – for example the complex calculations of his work on infinite geometric series – will help to clear any illusions the reader might have about the lack of sophistication among Hellenistic Greeks.

Perhaps the most well-known failure of the great scientist was not a failure of science, but of imagination. Archimedes was interested in the phenomenon of parallax – how different bodies in motion appear from different angles. When a fellow philosopher suggested that the Earth might revolve around the sun (instead of vice versa as generally believed), Archimedes shot down the idea by pointing out that angular parallax would put even the nearest stars at least tens of millions of miles away.

The mathematical breakthroughs of Archimedes created huge interest in the small circle of academics who regularly corresponded with each other across the known world, but what excited popular interest in the work of Archimedes were his mechanical inventions. One of these has probably been used by many a child at the fairground. This is the 'Archimedes claw' – a type of metal hand that is automatically forced closed by its own weight when it comes to rest upon an object. If dropped onto – for example – the prow of a ship, the claw could then be locked into place and winched up, taking the ship with it.

Of even more practical value was the device for moving water known today as the Archimedes screw. This screw was capable of pulling water upward through a pipe. It was – and still is – of great value in irrigation. In the early modern era it was noted that if an Archimedes screw could pull water one way, it could push it another. This fact became useful when such screws were mounted on the bottom of ships as a replacement for the more cumbersome paddle-wheel. In homage to the great scientist, the first screw-powered ship was called the SS *Archimedes* (launched in AD 1839).

Chapter 8

The Seleucid Empire

With Macedon, it is possible to make a number of statements about religion, language and customs, and be reasonably sure that, like the political system, these applied to the whole country. Likewise, in southern Greece, while the peninsula had a large number of cities, there was one common culture.

The Seleucid Empire was different because unlike, say, Syracuse, only a tiny part of this 'Hellenistic kingdom' was at all Hellenistic. The Seleucid Empire was vast and diverse and, outside cities, Greeks were nowhere a majority. Far from sharing a common culture, many of the peasants in some places in the Seleucid Empire were only vaguely aware that they were part of the empire at all, and they were unaware of even the existence of some of the other parts.

Thus we might have living side-by-side a fiercely monotheistic agricultural people whose administration was basically theocratic, and a polytheistic trading culture based around a number of independent cities. The two had different languages, alphabets and cultures. And alongside them was another polytheistic trading culture with a totally different pantheon, language and culture. That would be just the Levant, with the Jews, Phoenicians and Greeks. Then we go on to Mesopotamia, with the Elamites, Babylonians, and remnants of half a dozen other cultures, and so on.

While Macedon could be governed as a single nation state, because it was a single nation state, there was hardly a single thing about the Seleucid Empire which could be covered by a one-size-fits-all royal edict. As an empire the place was ungovernable. The only way that it could be governed was as the Persians had done and which the Seleucid kings wisely imitated. That was not to govern it as an empire at all, but as an untidy collection of kingdoms, statelets and tribal confederations. There was a reason why the Persian king had entitled himself as the 'king of kings'. This title was not so much an egoistical boast as a plain fact.

There were dozens of political and national entities within the Persian Empire which were ruled by their own king. Within his state, the king had pretty much the same powers of any other king, with the difference that instead of being the supreme ruler, the king had a king of his own. That king being the Persian shah, or the Seleucid ruler. Sometimes a local king was instead a high priest, or a Greek city council, but the idea was the same. Whatever administrative system the locals were accustomed to and would tolerate was generally accepted by the Seleucid Empire and left to get on with it, so long as the people paid their taxes and did not cause trouble by either rebelling or going to war with the neighbours.

This approach had weaknesses. The first was that while Macedonians felt Macedonian and Egyptians (generally, but in some cases fiercely) considered themselves Egyptian, few considered themselves 'Seleucid' for anything other than tax purposes. Many of the Seleucid kingdoms had little to bind them together other than that they shared a monarch who was foreign to each of them. Without a common language, culture or religion, and lacking any kind of nationalist sentiment, the Seleucid Empire was always an artificial and fissiparous construct.

Insofar as the empire had a common culture it was that of Greece, and it is to this extent that the kingdom could be called 'Hellenistic'. The ubiquity of Greek cities, especially after the assiduous city-building of Alexander and his successors, meant that few of the peoples of the empire were far from a Greek settlement. Since the Seleucid Empire's rulers were Greek, Greek was the language of administration, trade and increasingly the language that peoples from different parts of the empire used to talk to each other.

The language used in the Seleucid Empire was based on Ionic Greek, but after it had passed through the increasingly mongrel element of Alexander's Eastern armies this tongue had developed sufficient distinctive elements of its own to count as a separate dialect. Fittingly, this version of Greek is called *Koine* which means 'common'. It was the language used by a Phoenician businessman negotiating with a Pontic landowner for cedars which he planned to sell in Egypt. *Koine* is the type of Greek used in the original texts of the Bible and in the writings of many post–classical ancient historians. A version of *Koine* on the famous

Rosetta stone (now in the British Museum) was the key to allowing scholars to finally translate Egyptian hieroglyphs.

Because Hellenistic language and culture was one of the few common links binding together the disparate bits of the Seleucid Empire, local elites began adopting elements of this culture as a means of identifying with their rulers and also as a way of communicating with their peers across the empire. Over time this was to give rise to generations of 'Greeks' many of whose ancestors had never come within five hundred miles of the Greek mainland. Nevertheless, it is only recently that the Westernizing tendencies of euro-centric writers have been overcome, and the original Seleucid Empire seen as what it was – an empire of mainly Middle-Eastern peoples whose culture was leavened by an overall smattering of Greek culture.

The other unifying element in the empire was the king. All the different parts of the empire owed him fealty, and it was the king, either in person or through his personally selected administrators who held the whole thing together. To enforce the royal will, the king had his army which also was loyal to him in person. (Or rather the army was loyal to the monarchy. If on occasion the army felt a particular monarch was not up to scratch, they might kill him and replace him with a more suitable relative.)

To a large extent, the Seleucid Empire *was* the king. Subordinate rulers owed their fealty to the king rather than to the Seleucid state (whatever that might have been). This was a personal relationship, often confirmed by marriage ties, which meant that when a Seleucid king died, his successor had to laboriously go about re-establishing those relationships and creating new personal bonds. This was one reason why the death of a king was a particularly fraught time for the state. The other reason was because treaties between Hellenistic kings tended to be on the same basis. A peace treaty agreed between, for example, Ptolemy I and Seleucus I was not at all binding on their successors, which is why Ptolemy II felt free to go to war immediately after the death of his father.

Likewise, there were no career paths in what we might laughingly refer to as the Seleucid civil service. Doubtless there were clerks working among the lower ranks in offices in the Seleucid capitals tabulating tax returns and docketing land titles, but those in such jobs tended to stay there without change of status. There were also fewer of these than one might expect, because the federal nature of the empire meant that the minutiae of tax collection and other administration was handled by subordinate kings and city councils. The Seleucid administration itself simply specified what the tax take should be, and counted to make sure that the component states of the empire had paid it.

Higher ranks were selected on the basis of how well the administrators in question knew the king, and how competent, or loyal, the king knew that administrator to be. It was entirely at the royal whim whether the king would send someone to administer Babylon or Ephesus, and there was no fixed duration for such an appointment, nor an automatic promotion to another post thereafter. The king would consult with members of the imperial council, but the final decision was his alone. Likewise when the king was on the move (as he generally was), then it was up to petitioners and governors elsewhere in the empire to find him in order to get the royal judgement on outstanding matters. No fixed legislative body such as a senate ran things on a day-to-day basis from an imperial capital. The only source of final arbitration or new edicts was the king.

This administrative system, combined with a plethora of foreign enemies, meant that a Seleucid king was a sort of royal fire-fighter who spent most of his reign charging about the kingdom with his army dealing with crises both military and political – and these generally developed faster than they could be resolved. Furthermore, a wise king seldom delegated any significant administrative and military power to subordinates because such was the nature of the Seleucid Empire that an independent-minded general with enough soldiers could easily carve off a section of the empire for himself. In fact, taking Mesopotamia away from Perdiccas (pp.61 and 66) and holding it against Antigonus Monophthalmus was exactly how the first Seleucus had got started.

One result of this was that there was never really a Seleucid 'capital' in the way that Pella became the capital of Macedon or Alexandria was the capital of Egypt. There were administrative centres, such as Antioch in the west and Babylon or Seleucia in Mesopotamia, but most decision-making was done by the king and his council and these were far to busy to remain in any one place for long.

While the inherent problems of the Seleucid Empire never changed, running the place got easier over time. This was because crises which were considered less important or which developed in less-accessible parts of the empire were necessarily ignored by kings who had all the trouble they could handle right in their heartlands. Eventually these more distant crises became so acute that the region where they were happening dropped out of Seleucid control altogether, thus leaving the king with one less problem area to worry about.

As we have seen, the place where this happened first and fastest was the far east of the kingdom, and it is there to which we now turn.

Bactria, Sogdiana and the Indian kingdoms

This huge region took up parts of modern Iran, Afghanistan, Pakistan and Turkmenistan. It was the last part of Alexander's empire to be conquered, and among the first to go. It was also the part of Alexander's empire that most fiercely resisted conquest in the first place. The cultural differences between the Greeks and local peoples created more strain here than elsewhere, since, for example, the monotheistic fire-worshipping Sogdians were appalled by the Greek tradition of desecrating fire by using it to burn the bodies of the dead. The locals were also appalled by the large number of Greek settlers in the region.

This settlement actually in some cases predated Alexander's conquests, as the Persian kings had found the far east of their empire a handy place to dump rebellious Greeks from cities under their control in Asia Minor. Thereafter Alexander greatly increased the number of exiles by forcibly retiring some of his veteran soldiers to new cities strategically placed to hold down dissent. Because they had little choice about having been placed in this distant land, many Sogdian and Bactrian Greeks no more wanted to be there than the locals wanted them to stay. When Alexander died, many of these reluctant settlers tried to return to the West and had to be sent 'home' by force.

One of the problems for Alexander's successors was that these far eastern domains were very far away. Between Antioch in Syria and Samarkand in Sogdiana stretched 3,500 kilometres (2,175 miles) of mountain and desert. A king in a hurry could get there in just under three months provided he did not take an army with him. Since anything that did require the presence of the king that urgently probably did require the army also, that took the journey up to four months. This meant that, even if the king turned around as soon as he reached his destination, the Syrian heartland of the empire would be left to fend for itself for eight months. That was a long time to be away when armies of the Macedonians, the Galatians and the interfering Ptolemy II were much, much closer.

The pragmatic Seleucus considered the problem and quickly decided that the situation in the east was untenable. Either he was to become an Eastern king governing Alexander's Indian conquests and leaving the West to others, or he would become a Syria-based monarch, which necessarily meant abandoning the least defensible of Alexander 's eastern conquests. The result was something of a territorial fire-sale to the nearest Indian monarch. In exchange Seleucus got the war elephants which were instrumental in winning the Battle of Ipsus (p.72) and his future empire, so perhaps Seleucus considered the loss of his Indian domains well worth it for the price he got for them.

The Greeks in India generally remained in place despite the change of ruler. Many of them occupied comfortable trades or estates and their native ruler – as was often also the case elsewhere – was more than satisfied with his productive foreign subjects. With the passing of time and the slow decay of the Seleucid Empire, the Indo-Greek population lost touch with their Hellenistic roots and slowly merged with the Indian peoples among whom they lived. Nevertheless, the fused Indo-Greek culture was itself dynamic and would retain its distinctive character for centuries to come.

Even having divested himself of his Indian possessions, this still left the Seleucid king the question of how to govern the remaining and very substantial domains of Sogdiana and Bactria.

One solution was to try to govern the east of the empire from still-distant but at least somewhat-closer Mesopotamia. This worked for Seleucus because he trusted his son, the future Antiochus I, whose mother was Sogdian anyway. In later years, once Antiochus became king he attempted the same solution with his eldest son. This eldest son (also called Seleucus) promptly demonstrated the flaw in the system, which was that the job of running the east properly needed administrative and military resources sufficient for an independent kingdom. Antiochus eventually executed his son in the belief that this independent kingdom was exactly what the son had in mind.

Nevertheless, Antiochus was aware at first hand of the difficulties which his eastern possessions faced. They were at the interface between the wild tribes which roamed the steppe to the north and the agricultural communities to the south. Consequently Sogdiana was constantly subject to huge barbarian raids. One such, in the 280s BC required a major intervention by Antiochus before it was repelled. Thereafter Antiochus again tried to strengthen the region's defences, partly by bringing in yet more Greek settlers.

Bactria was a wealthy region well worth hanging on to if the Seleucid monarchs could only work out how to do it. The country sat squarely across the famed Silk Road, and indeed had largely contributed to that road's creation thanks to the domestication of the famous double-humped Bactrian camel. Tough and tireless, the Bactrian camel could get by with a small amount of water while carrying loads over distances that would leave even the hardiest of mules choking in its dust.

Greek culture was becoming well-established in the region, though it was a largely urban culture. Still, there was quite a lot of urbanism. The later writer Justin talks of 'Bactria of the thousand cities' (Justin 41.4). This is doubtless an exaggeration, even if we count – as Justin doubtless did – a 'city' as any semi-autonomous collection of buildings which had its own governing council.

Nevertheless, Bactria was wealthy and vast – well over the size of modern Germany and France combined. The native religion of Zoroastrianism and the Olympic Pantheon of the Greeks between them produced a degree of intellectual ferment which led to a rise in Buddhism, a religion/philosophy which had been around since the 5th century BC, but which only really began to expand at around this time.

The problem for the Seleucid kings was that, as we have seen, the more the Greeks interacted with the native Bactrian people, and the two languages and cultures found common ground between them, the more separate and isolated from the remainder of the Seleucid Empire the Bactrians felt themselves to be. In the 260s BC the administrator of

Bactria and Sogdiana was a man called Diodotus. The current Seleucid king – Antiochus II – had attempted to claim the man's loyalty by giving him his daughter in marriage. It was not enough. Once Bactria became isolated from the rest of the Seleucid Empire by a rebellion in Parthia to the west, Diodotus declared Bactria-Sogdiana (together with what remnants of their Indian possessions the Seleucids still held) as a separate kingdom, with himself as King Diodotus I.

From our point of view, this marks the creation of yet another 'Hellenistic' kingdom (for a given definition of 'Hellenistic'), and it was rather a successful one at that. It was to outlast its Western counterparts and eventually merge with the Indo-Greek kingdom and last well into the Roman era.

Mesopotamia

In terms of royal reach, Mesopotamia was about as far as the power of a Seleucid king could stretch. Even then this was not easy, for travel between Syria and Mesopotamia is difficult (especially if accompanied by an army) and limited to a few routes.

The Mesopotamian command included the highlands of what is now modern Iran. The peoples living there had impressed Alexander with their fighting ability, and he eagerly tried to recruit them into his armies. Despite Alexander's attempts to merge his Macedonians with the Iranians the two cultures remained distinct, with even the top rank of Iranian aristocrats acquiring only a patina of Hellenization. Recognizing this, the Seleucids tried to control the area through dynastic links with leading Iranian families rather than the strategically-placed city foundations which they used elsewhere.

The Parthians, and the Medians who occupied a neighbouring region, were always more than somewhat independent minded, and as soon as Antiochus became deeply embroiled in struggles with Ptolemaic Egypt, his satrap, Andragoras, promptly rebelled. He may have synchronized his rebellion with that of Diodotus, for the Seleucid Empire lost this huge swathe of its eastern domains within a few years (247–245 BC).

While Andragoras never formally declared himself king, he did issue coins showing himself sporting a royal diadem. He may have regretted bailing out of the Seleucid Empire when he did, because soon afterwards his lands were attacked by a migratory tribe called the Parni. The Parni were an Indo-European people from around the southern shores of the Caspian Sea, though there are indications that they originated from even further north and west. Andragoras was killed in the struggle with the invaders who now settled in the region, merged with the native peoples, and became the Parthians. These Parthians were to gradually take over much of the eastern Seleucid domains in the century which followed.

Mesopotamia had for centuries been dominated by the city of Babylon. Babylon was already some 1,600 years old when Alexander added the city to his empire. At the time it was one of the largest cities in the world, with a population estimated at between 100,000 to 200,000 people. The city was on the River Euphrates and had long been the administrative centre for the lands around. The Persians conquered Babylon in the sixth century, but did nothing to dent the city's reputation as a centre of scholarship, especially in the disciplines of astronomy/astrology and mathematics.

It was not Alexander, but Seleucus Nicator who dealt Babylon a blow from which it never really recovered. Seleucus took note of the entrenched power of the priests in Babylon and the city's penchant for rebellion. (Babylon had constantly resisted the power of Assyria when that empire was dominant, and had rebelled several times against Persian rule also.) Therefore, in 305 Seleucus set about building himself a city deliberately – though not explicitly – designed to rival Babylon. The city was called Seleucia, but due to an abundance of other Seleuciae founded everywhere from Sogdiana to Gaza, this particular city is generally called Seleucia-on-the-Tigris. In contrast to Babylon's ancient and entrenched institutions, this Seleucia was designed from the start as a Hellenistic city, with temples, gymnasia and the other accoutrements of Greek urban civilization. The foundation on the Tigris, though not far from Babylon also had a strategic purpose. While operating from Mesopotamia Seleucus had endured invasions from both Antigonus Monophthalmus and his son and was well aware that the region's defences needed shoring up against attack from that direction.

Seleucus would ideally have liked to stock his new city with young Greeks and Macedonians, preferably craftsmen, merchants and peasants with military training. However, there were precious few Greeks to go around, partly because the original stock came from a relatively small and underpopulated country, and partly because it was equally imperative for the Seleucids to populate their new cities in Syria, which were under constant threat from the other Hellenistic kingdoms, but especially Egypt.

As a result, Seleucia-on-the-Tigris became exactly what the Babylonian priests had feared from the start it would be – a sort of vampire twin to Babylon which drained manpower and administrative roles from the ancient city. By the Roman period, writers such as Strabo and Diodorus described Babylon as largely deserted, with the population living in one corner and growing their crops within the city walls. By the time of Trajan, the city was an abandoned ruin (Cassius Dio 68.30.1). Meanwhile Seleucia went on to become one of the great cities of the Hellenistic world, and was still going strong while the Roman Empire in the West collapsed.

Apart from the urbanized area between the Euphrates and the Tigris, the region of Mesopotamia had also separate administrative areas which ranged from medium-sized kingdoms to the traditional pastures of semi-nomadic tribes. The largest of these areas was what is partly the state of modern Armenia today, though under the Seleucids this was divided into smaller administrative units such as Sophene (in modern Turkey) as well as Armenia itself.

Syria

In ancient terms 'Syria' was a more encompassing description than the area occupied by the modern state. At its most general Syria was the region stretching from the River Orontes and the Anti-Taurus Mountains in the north, along the banks of the Euphrates to the east and the shores of the Mediterranean to the west until one comes to the gates of Egypt in Gaza.

This was a geographically and culturally diverse area which contained a number of Semitic peoples, mainly the Jews, Arabs and Phoenicians. It was also largely underpopulated in parts, due both to climatic conditions unfavourable to agriculture and the region's age-old propensity for warfare which hindered agriculture even in those areas where it was practicable.

Seleucus Nicator took possession of Syria after the Battle of Ipsus, and immediately began transforming the area into the foundation stone of his empire. Immediately after the division of the Macedonian Empire after Ipsus, Seleucus did not have possession of the southern 'empty' portion, which Ptolemy I had grabbed. Seleucus certainly felt he was entitled to that part as well, and over the next century or so the Seleucid and Ptolemaic kingdoms fought over the area like dogs over a bone.

The most Hellenized part of Syria lay to the northwest, and was centred on Antioch. Again, this city is sometimes called Antioch-on-the-Orontes, because Seleucus founded several such cities (named after his father, Antiochus), and his son and successor (also Antiochus) founded several more as well, making sixteen Antiochi in all. There is a possibly apocryphal story that the choice of location for this particular Antioch was left to the gods. An eagle (sacred to Zeus) was given a hunk of meat sanctified by sacrifice. A group of keen-eyed priests watched the eagle fly off with the meat and the city was founded where the bird settled to consume his meal.

This turned out to be on Mount Silipus on the banks of the Orontes, which shows that the eagle knew a thing or two about where to locate a city. Silipus proved to be a useful location for the city's acropolis. The banks of the Orontes were an excellent site for the rest of the city, and the river itself provided water, sewage disposal and a trade route. The Orontes rises in the Lebanon, flows across the fertile plain upon which Antioch was situated and then flows southeast through the gorge of Tempe before meeting the sea just south of another Seleucid foundation, Seleucia Pieria. While the Orontes was not easily navigable, the advantages of water transport still made Antioch a useful terminus of the Silk Road. This route now ran through the Seleucid Empire for almost a third of its length, bringing spices from India, silk from China and much else, greatly enriching merchants and towns all along the way.

Overall, there were four great Seleucid cities in Syria, which were known in antiquity as the Syrian Tetrapolis. These formed the innermost core of the empire. Antioch (now Antakya in modern Turkey) we have already met, likewise Seleucia Pieria on the coast which combined a very good defensive location with an even better harbour. Apamea, named after one of the wives of Seleucus, was also on the Orontes, and almost enclosed by one of the loops of the river. (The twisting path of this river lay behind the Greek legend that it was formed when the coils of a huge dragon-snake fell from the sky after a battle with the gods. The weight of the coils dented the land into the later path of the river.) Coming equipped with a pre-built massive moat made Apamea a natural fortress site, and it was here that the Seleucids housed their formidable regiments of war elephants.

Near Apamea stood Laodicea, though exactly which of the Laodices in the Seleucid family bestowed the city with her name is uncertain. (It is certainly a matter of regret that the Hellenistic kings were so utterly unoriginal in their naming practices.) The mountain behind the city was eventually cultivated into vineyards reaching almost to the summit, and these provided wines for which the city became famous.

In the south, the land was already dominated by the great Phoenician cities of Tyre, Byblos, Sidon and Aradus, though Tyre was still less the city that it had once been as it was slowly recovering from the rough handling it had been given in the process of being captured by Alexander the Great. The Seleucid kings left the Phoenician cities as autonomous units, content to collect a handy tax from the cities' mercantile activities.

Less useful from a Seleucid point of view were the peoples of Judea in their harsh inland settlements. The problem with the Jews was not so much their religion, because the empire contained many different religions, some monotheistic, others animist and some polytheistic.

Rather the issue was Jewish nationalism. In a world in which most peoples were somewhat relaxed about what state they lived in, the people of Judea insisted ferociously on belonging to themselves. They regarded foreign rule as an imposition to be thrown off as rapidly as possible. In the past the Jews had opposed Assyrians, Neo-Babylonians, Egyptians and Persians. Consequently they had honed being awkward and recalcitrant subjects into almost an art form.

Being well aware of this, and with plenty of other problems to deal with, the Seleucids would have been happy to do as they did elsewhere in their empire, which was step back and let the Jews rule themselves. The problem was that the Jews were not very good at self-rule either, and the country was in a constant state of political and religious ferment.

The Seleucid army

As has been argued above, the main factors which held the Seleucid Empire together were the king, and the veneer of Hellenism which gave the upper classes of the empire a common bond. Without these unifying forces, the efforts of the army would have been in vain. Nevertheless, the Seleucid army was fundamental in maintaining the integrity of the empire and did so through its very basic function of invading the country of any ruler with separatist intentions.

While the army was good at this, and got better over time, the essential problem is summarized in the term 'the Seleucid army'. A moment's thought would suggest that in so massive an empire, with enemies or potential enemies on every side, what was required were several Seleucid armies. Yet, apart from garrison forces, by and large the empire made do with one field army.

Strategically, this made no sense. Politically it was essential. The purpose of the army was to enforce the king's will. To make sure that this is what it did, the army was under the personal command of the king, and when the army was on campaign – as it almost always was – the king was in personal command. If the empire were to raise another army of a size enough to be useful, then whoever was placed in command of that army would immediately start getting ideas about setting himself up as king in the area of the empire that his army commanded. That is pretty much what Diodotus I did in Bactria, and what in later years various other breakaway leaders did as soon as they felt that they possessed enough military force to get away with it.

Therefore, having two large armies within the empire almost guaranteed that sooner or later these two armies would end up cancelling each other out in a civil war. As a result there was just the one Seleucid army to deal with an empire's worth of problems. Should that army be tied up in combat with for example, the Egyptians, then while that conflict was in progress a backlog of issues would begin to pile up which the army would need to deal with as soon as the Egyptian war was resolved.

In a nutshell, that was the fundamental flaw with the early Seleucid Empire. Only the king and his army could resolve issues that needed a military solution. There were far too many such issues, and they usually happened simultaneously in places far apart from each other. Yet the Seleucid king could only tackle them one at a time. The Seleucid army was a serial solution to parallel problems.

The centrifugal tendency of the empire – that, is the tendency for the empire's component parts to fly apart – was also the reason why the Seleucid kings were reluctant to raise levies from the native peoples. While an army of Armenians would probably do a good job of defending Armenia, they would do an equally good job of defending an independent Armenia against the Seleucid army. Indeed, once the Parthians had broken away from the empire it was the competence of their army that prevented the Seleucids from re-integrating them. The last thing the Seleucid kings wanted was native peoples from elsewhere in the empire acquiring the same military ability. Yet shortages of manpower sometimes forced them to recruit native troops in any case.

The Seleucid army was composed mainly of Greeks, Macedonians and a good smattering of Thracians. As with settlers, merchants and craftsmen, the Seleucids could never get enough soldiers (even though the empire's efforts to do so were rapidly depopulating mainland Greece). Therefore as well as native levies, mercenaries were often added to supplement the army's numbers.

The Seleucids operated a sort of feudal system with suitable immigrants from Greece. Settlers were allocated to cities, as the *polis* was the structure with which most new arrivals were familiar. As was the age-old pattern in Greece, these settlers farmed land immediately outside the city. Even the many farmers who were permanently domiciled on their lands (those closest to the city did their farming as commuters) had the city as their administrative and religious centre. When the king needed soldiers each city was required to supply a certain number. Those who were called up for military service were well aware that this might happen as it was in return for the promise of such service that they had been given land in the first place.

Contemporary historians do not record what happened to the native peoples who were moved off the farmlands that the new cities came to occupy. This was in part because these historians were not greatly interested in small communities of peasant farmers, but also because the consequences were less severe than they might be in the modern world. With the press of twenty-first century humanity, almost all land that can be usefully farmed is farmed. However, two thousand years ago humans were still comparatively rare, and even in places like long-settled Mesopotamia, land could be found for fairly large-scale population transfers. In the case of Seleucid city foundations this was even easier as many of the original peoples found themselves co-opted into becoming (second-class) citizens of a new city.

The Hellenistic armies of Macedon, Egypt and the Seleucid Empire were not radically different from the army of Alexander the Great. Though the kings experimented with different ideas, from elephants and camels to catapults, the two basic elements of the army remained the phalanx and the cavalry.

The phalanx was a deadly instrument of war. If it was on suitable ground and all the long spears (*sarissae*) of the phalangites were pointed in the right direction, then the only thing capable of stopping a phalanx was another phalanx. (This remained true until it was proven that a Roman legion could do the same job. Even then, Aemilius Paulus, the general who did the demonstrating admitted that the memory of the phalanx advancing toward him, pointy end first, sometimes woke him up sweating at nights.)

The pikes of the phalangites were slightly longer than those used by earlier Macedonian armies, and alongside the phalanx might be found a levy of whatever native troops were available, from Syrian bowmen to Iranian cavalry to naked Galatian warriors. Another type which gained in popularity in this era was the mercenary peltast. Often this was a Thracian, though other Greek communities such as the Aetolians were also warming to the concept. Whereas the members of the phalanx were very much components of a complex formation and almost defenceless as individuals, peltasts tended to fight in loose *ad hoc* formations which took maximum advantage of whatever terrain they were fighting on.

Peltasts were lightly armoured, often with just a helmet, since mobility was more essential to their role than staying power in combat. Their distinctive item of equipment was the *pelte*. This was a shield, often crescent shaped, which gave the troop type its name. The shield had a loose strap which meant that it could be slung over the peltast's back while he was retreating, this allowing extra mobility while protecting his rear.

Weaponry was highly varied, and seems to have depended on the individual and the situation. Generally the peltast carried several javelins, and often a longer spear. This longer spear was to discourage cavalry rather than for set-piece fighting in a battle-line. When it did come to close combat with other light infantry, the peltast's preferred weapon was a sword.

Generally, the function of peltasts in battle was to cover any loose ground that the more densely-packed phalanx could not operate on. Additionally peltasts provided the link between calvary and infantry on the battleground. A further reason for using peltasts in an army was because while set-piece battles tended to be few and far between, skirmishes, patrols and other regular activities of an army in the field were best carried out by peltasts or cavalry.

When it came to cavalry, the Seleucids were spoiled for choice. The Seleucids developed a taste for a type of very heavily armoured cavalryman called the cataphract (which literally means 'covered over' – for not only were the riders armoured from top to bottom, but so were their horses). During the Persian wars the Greeks had tended to denigrate this cavalry type, because cataphracts were slow and could make little impression against a formed battle-line of spearmen. In later years though, the Seleucids found them very useful against more irregular troops. The Galatians fought in a looser formation, and once cataphracts got in among them a rout generally followed, and being almost impervious to long-range bow fire, cataphracts provided a useful screen.

Cataphracts were basically very heavy infantry on hooves, but Seleucid kings could also call on Sarmatian lancers, and (until they took matters into their own hands and broke away from the empire) the superb Iranian heavy cavalry. The richer Greeks and Macedonians provided the Companion cavalry, which was usually the unit in which the king himself fought. From there, cavalry became lighter, and included the fine skirmishing horsemen of Cappadocia, and the famed horse archers from the east. (Two centuries later, these horse archers were to be instrumental in wiping out the Roman legions at Carrhae, as the legions had no answer to their form of warfare.)

Thus the Seleucid army really did find strength in diversity. Assuming the right units were available at a given time, the army's flexibility and variety of troop types could be used to great advantage against more limited foes. Facing Galatian invaders? Use dromedary units on camels to scare off Gallic horses unused to the smell, then send cataphracts around the back of the infantry while at the front ploughing into their loose formations with the phalanx. Egyptians? Use light cavalry to discombobulate their chariots, cataphracts to disperse the bowmen, and an elephant charge to disperse the native levies. Then skirmish across the front of the phalanx to wear it down with peltasts, and finally bring in the Seleucid phalanx to finish the job.

Overall, the Seleucid army was a well-practised and highly effective instrument of war. With three more armies like it and the political will at the top, the Seleucid Empire might have survived.

Chapter 9

Ptolemaic Egypt

As an integrated nation-state, Macedon had been in existence for around a century and a half before the reign of Alexander the Great. As an integrated kingdom, Egypt had existed for around three thousand years before that. Even today the 60-metre-high Pyramid of Djoser, built twenty-five centuries before the birth of Alexander, reminds us that the Ptolemaic rule of Egypt was but a fleeting moment in the long history of that land. It is also worth noting that of the Seven Wonders of the ancient world, only two were non-Greek – the Great Pyramid at Giza and The Hanging Gardens of Babylon. The Great Pyramid was the oldest of all the Wonders and it is now the last survivor of the Seven.

The Egyptians were very conscious of their long history, and bitterly resented it when their long history of independence came to an end in 525 BC with the country's conquest by the Persians. Three years later, the Egyptians rebelled. They rebelled again in 486 BC, and again in 460 BC (this time with Athenian help). Then they rebelled in 411 BC in an extended rebellion that succeeded in ejecting the Persians from the country altogether. This was the last time in ancient history that Egypt was an independent country. In 343 BC the Persians regained control of Egypt just in time to yield it to the conquering armies of Alexander the Great.

This history of Egyptian rebellions would have been uppermost in the mind of Ptolemy I Soter when he took control of the country. It might even have been one of his primary reasons for taking Egypt out of what at the time was the still-intact empire of Alexander the Great. If Egyptians so hated the idea of being controlled by a foreign power, it was worth demonstrating that their ruler, even if a foreigner, was at least their ruler and theirs alone.

Over the centuries that followed, there remained a slightly schizophrenic flavour to Ptolemaic rule. To the outside world, the Ptolemies were not only Greek, but uber-Greeks – leaders in Hellenic arts, science, architecture and culture. Yet south of Alexandria, the Ptolemies were depicted as being more Egyptian in appearance, custom and religious devotion than the most Egyptian of the native Pharaohs. It was a difficult double act, and one which the Ptolemies did not always pull off successfully. There was unrest and there were a number of rebellions. Yet the surprising thing was not that these rebellions happened, but how rarely they happened, and their relatively muted scale when they did.

Geography

Apart from the Egyptian heartlands, the Ptolemaic kingdom at times extended to places one does not usually consider Egyptian, such as Cyprus and Damascus. Indeed, at times the Egyptian kingdom included much of the Levant and parts of southern Anatolia. To the west, 'Egypt' included the formerly independent Cyrenaica and the four Greek cities of Cyrene and Barca, together with the new foundations of Ptolemais and Berenice (this Berenice was different to the city mentioned on p.92 which was at the other side of the kingdom on the shores of the Red Sea). One would imagine that these extensive overseas possessions helped Ptolemy I's internal propaganda, for Egyptian rule had not been so extensive since the time of the revered Ramesses II of Egypt's 19th Dynasty, who had lived a thousand years before.

Egypt proper remained as it had been for millennia, two kingdoms with a single ruler. Upper Egypt was more insular, and though there were Greek cities, the region never became Hellenistic to the same degree as the north. Due to its connection with the Mediterranean world, Lower Egypt was always the richer and more cosmopolitan of the two kingdoms but it never subsumed its southern neighbour. Thus we see the Ptolemaic Pharaohs depicted with the red crown of Lower Egypt, and the white crown of Upper Egypt, holding both the papyrus, symbol of the lower kingdom, and the reed, symbol of the upper. Egyptian crowns sometimes show the vulture, which was sacred in Upper Egypt. The British Museum has a surviving bust of Ptolemy I as pharaoh wearing a head-dress with the cobra associated with the goddess Wadjet, a protector deity of Lower Egypt.

Upper Egypt started south of the ancient kingdom of Kush, close to the Tropic of Cancer at Abu Simel near the first cataract of the Nile. This is a site famous both in Ptolemaic and modern times for the massive temple complex which was cut into a cliff in the time of Ramesses II. Here, the island fortress town of Elephantine was protected by the ram-headed God Khnum. Khnum had to share his island with foreign deities, for as early as the fifth century BC the island was home to a colony of Jewish mercenaries. In later years a Greek contingent seems to have joined them.

During the Middle (c.2050–1700 BC) and New Kingdoms (c.1600–1100 BC) the capital of the kingdom was in Upper Egypt at the city of Thebes. Not that the place was called 'Thebes' at the time, as the proper name can be transliterated to something like 'Waseet'. However, the Greeks seem to have associated the city with Thebes because they also associated the city's deity Shu with Hercules, and Hercules came from the Greek Thebes. So the Greek name of Thebes is the one that stuck in later centuries. The existence of an Egyptian Hercules was already well established in Greek minds by the time of Herodotus, and is just one of many links between early Greece and Egypt. (In fact Hercules had his own city of Heraklepolis further up the Nile.)

Lower Egypt had a profusion of cities, each under its own tutelary deity. There was for example Letopolis (Ausim) dedicated to Horus, and Bubastis (Per-Bast) which was the centre of worship for Bastet the Goddess of Cats. The political centre of the north was at Memphis, the capital of the Old Kingdom (c. 2500 – 2100 BC) though in the Ptolemaic era this city was totally eclipsed by Alexandria.

(The reason why most ancient Egyptian cities have both Greek-style names and an Egyptian alternative is because, until hieroglyphics became comprehensible in AD 1822, all that scholars had to go on were the Greek and Roman names for these places. By the time the proper names were known, changing to these would have involved editing dozens of texts and re-educating hundreds of scholars. The process is now under way, but even 200 years later, it is a slow business.)

Climatically Egypt is hard desert. Lycopolis (modern Asyut) was more or less in the middle of Ptolemaic Egypt and the city's annual rainfall is essentially 0.0 mm. (0.0 inches). Temperatures can soar to the 40s centigrade (over 100 degrees Fahrenheit), and huge dust storms sweep the region. The only reason that the country is inhabitable is because apart from a few oases, all water comes from the Nile. In fact it would be fair to say that for Egypt all life came from the Nile. Every year the Goddess Isis remembered the death of her husband Osiris, and she wept so profusely that the Nile overflowed, flooding the fields alongside with rich black silt.

Alternatively one might prefer the more boring modern explanation that the annual monsoon dumps enormous quantities of rainfall into the Ethiopian highlands and these waters come south, bearing with them in the form of silt a good quantity of Ethiopia which has been eroded away in the process. The flooding of the Nile was a major event in Egyptian life. When the floods failed – and they did several times in the Ptolemaic era due to volcanic action interfering with the monsoons – huge political and economic stress resulted. In fact modern research has shown that the failure of the Nile flood at times forced the Ptolemies to make peace with their Seleucid rivals to concentrate upon the internal crisis which followed. (J. Manning et al. 'Volcanic suppression of Nile summer flooding triggers revolt and constrains interstate conflict in ancient Egypt', *Nature Communications*, 2017).

Trade and Economy

One of the reasons why Ptolemaic Egypt was a power in the Mediterranean world was that the Ptolemies were highly proactive in developing their new homeland as an economic power. While a general of Alexander, Ptolemy I Soter had seen for himself the river of wealth that flowed westward along the Silk Road. He wanted a substantial cut of that for Egypt, and worked hard to get it. His son and successor Ptolemy II was very much on board with the project, and the pair managed to build in a fork into the Silk Road when it reached India. At that point, thanks largely to the efforts of the first Ptolemies, many merchants chose to take their goods south for shipping from Indian ports across the Red Sea to

Egypt. There such goods which were destined for onward traffic were brought down the Nile to Alexandria which – as always intended – had grown into a major port.

Alexandria also acted as a trade corridor for goods such as ivory which were exported from Kush and even deeper in Africa. These goods were bundled with papyrus and linen as exports to the wider world. (Despite a number of attempts, no-one succeeded in large-scale papyrus production outside Egypt, though one small but flourishing crop grew at the Fountain of Arethusa on the 'island' of Ortygia in Syracuse.)

Thanks to the rich silt brought by the Nile flood, Egypt usually had a surplus of wheat which was exported abroad. In Roman times the city of Rome was famously dependent on Egyptian wheat, but well before then the Ptolemies had started exploring new markets for Egyptian wheat.

In Alexandria and a series of towns both along the Nile and in the delta, workmen produced the country's signature glass vases, which were opaque, but vividly coloured, and also faience vessels. Faience is a type of ceramic with a glass glaze that produces a fine deep colour. The result is somewhere between glassware and pottery and in ancient times this was a prestige product elsewhere in the Mediterranean. The fondness of Egyptians for a particularly lustrous shade of blue led to this colour becoming known as 'Egyptian Blue'.

Some Greek towns such as Naucratis had long been established in Egypt (there are indications that Greek traders worked out of Naucratis even in Mycenaean times). Nevertheless the first Ptolemies encouraged the development of new towns and the arrival of Greek settlers for exactly the same reason that the Seleucids did – they wanted Greek military manpower. These settlers were given the same terms as those who moved to Seleucid towns – land in exchange for a commitment to military service. While many of the Greek settlers in Egypt chose to live in the Nile Delta, several substantial Greek towns also developed along the Nile.

The first Ptolemies

With the Egyptian dynasty the unimaginative Macedonian naming convention was taken to its logical extreme with every male king being called Ptolemy. In the end they went through fourteen iterations of the name from Ptolemy I to Ptolemy XIV, though a case can be made for a fifteenth Ptolemy, who was the son of Julius Caesar and Cleopatra (the seventh), though this son is generally known today as Caesarion.

The trend-setter was Ptolemy I Soter. Given the links we have seen between Egypt and Hercules it comes as no surprise to discover that as soon as he became pharaoh, Ptolemy made much of his claim to that hero as one of his ancestors. He set about identifying his dynasty with Egypt and succeeded so thoroughly that even today many people are surprised to discover that Cleopatra – the last of the line – was not Egyptian but pure-bred Greek.

Once he had taken Egypt, Ptolemy never left the country again. To the Egyptians Ptolemy tried to appear as just another native pharaoh. Rather than adopt a policy of Hellenization and make the Egyptians more Greek, Ptolemy (outside Alexandria) worked hard to be Egyptian. Not only was the age-old Egyptian religion allowed to continue, it was strongly promoted. The first Ptolemies enthusiastically supported Egyptian cults, and tended to rule through the Egyptian priesthood, just as their native predecessors had done. As the country became wealthier under their careful guidance, the Ptolemies put in place a programme of temple restoration and construction.

So extensive was this that most of the surviving Egyptian temples today are from the Ptolemaic era. Yet so closely did the Ptolemies follow established convention that few tourists exploring these temples today realize that they were actually built by Greek kings who employed Greek craftsmen. Even in Alexandria, which was consciously designed as a Hellenistic city, there were Egyptian temples. Some of these were also dedicated to the royal cult. In Egypt generally, but in Alexandria particularly, Ptolemy encouraged the worship of the god Serapis.

While Serapis may have existed before, it was Ptolemy who raised a previously obscure god to one of the major deities of the state. Serapis became a replacement husband for the goddess Isis – an Egyptian goddess who, thanks also to aggressive Ptolemaic promotion, was now gaining traction and worshippers in the wider Greek world. Serapis was a fully syncretized deity. By, for example, insisting that this particular Egyptian god had a human rather than an animal head, Ptolemy made the god acceptable to Greek worshippers. (In fact both Serapis and Isis long outlasted Ptolemaic Egypt and were finally suppressed by Christian Roman emperors at the end of the fourth century AD.) Temples to Serapis were called Serapeums. Apart from a very famous such temple in Alexandria, the remains of others can still be found today in (among other places) Hadrian's Villa and the Quirinal Hill in Rome, and also in Pergamon, Miletus and Ephesus in the Greek East.

Ptolemy I was responsible for putting in motion the measures which were to make Alexandria the cultural centre of the Hellenistic world. Though he did not live long enough to see many of the new developments to their conclusion, his work was built upon (in many cases literally) by Ptolemy II and his successors.

We know that Ptolemy I set the tone personally by writing a history of the campaigns of Alexander. Though this history is now lost, much of the content survives in Arrian's *History of Alexander* (the *Anabasis*), for Arrian explicitly says that he used Ptolemy as one of his major sources. Apparently Ptolemy strove to follow the objectivity of the great Athenian historian Thucydides, but like Thucydides, Ptolemy could not resist getting in some digs at characters whose names he felt deserved to be blackened for posterity. Particularly Ptolemy was at pains to show Perdiccas as an unworthy successor to Alexander, and to thus make more excusable his own role in breaking up Alexander's empire by making Egypt independent.

Ptolemy I also started the trend of inviting the most distinguished scholars and philosophers of the ancient world to take up residence in Egypt. His first major catch was Euclid, perhaps the most influential mathematician of all time. Euclid surpasses even the genius of Archimedes in this regard, because his *Elements of Geometry* holds the record for any school textbook, having been in continuous use for the torture of schoolchildren from the start of the third century BC until the end of the nineteenth century AD.

In a probably apocryphal tale (the first recorded telling is by Proculus, six hundred years later), Ptolemy I found the *Elements* as baffling as hundreds of generations of schoolchildren were later to do. He appealed to Euclid to make his explanations a touch simpler, but was brushed off with the reply, 'Sire, there is no Royal Road to Geometry' – which is usually misquoted today as 'There is no Royal Road to Knowledge.'

The Great Library

Another recruit to Ptolemy I's intellectual army was Demetrius of Phalerum. The multi-talented Demetrius was an orator, a philosopher, a scholar and an administrator who ran the city of Athens for ten years as an appointee of Cassander. Demetrius introduced a number of useful reforms to the Athenian legal system, but was kicked out when Demetrios the son of Antigonus Monophthalmus captured the city. Informed that he would be executed if he ever tried to return, Demetrius of Phalerum eventually made his way to the court of Ptolemy I.

Ptolemy first employed the legal talents of Demetrius in fine-tuning the legal system he planned for the kingdom. Afterwards, Ptolemy noted Demetrius' fondness for literary criticism, and decided that this, combined with the man's administrative abilities, would make him a superb librarian. The library was to be in Alexandria, naturally, and, rather like Alexandria itself, it was planned from the beginning on a monumental scale. The library's far-from-modest mission was to be the repository of all human knowledge. Libraries had existed before, but these were mostly for the preservation of particular texts – such as the Babylonian astronomical library – or preserving works from a particular area. For example the Athenian library had only texts from Attic authors. The Library at Alexandria was the first library to want to collect all information from everyone, everywhere. Even then, the library was intended as but one part of an even greater whole.

That greater whole was a very expanded Temple of the Muses. In that temple were stored artefacts useful for the generation of knowledge, one of which was the collection of books in the Library. Just as a temple of Serapis was called a Serapaeum, a temple of the Muses was called a Musaeum. The function of the Musaeum of Alexandria has since been replicated in museums across the world. (And it was a moment of particular regret to Hellenistic scholars when the British Library was moved away from the British Museum, where previously the pair had replicated the dual role of the Alexandrian Museum and Library.)

As a result of the museum/library combination, the overall complex was a sort of proto-university, complete with faculties (including Philosophy, Anatomy, Astronomy, Physics and Engineering), visiting professors and tenured staff. The gains for the Ptolemies were practical – for example when Ptolemy wanted a canal between the Red Sea and the Nile he had the finest minds in the known world on hand to conduct a feasibility study. (Which concluded that the difference in water levels exposed the Nile to a potentially catastrophic salt–water flood. When the canal was eventually built, a system of sophisticated locks and fail-safes was added to prevent this.)

In less tangible terms, the Museum and Library shifted Egypt from an oddball relic at the periphery to the centre of intellectualism in the Hellenic world. To have studied at the Library gave any would-be scholar instant credibility from Bactria to Spain, and as a result Ptolemaic Egypt became the acknowledged torch-bearer of Hellenistic thought.

It is uncertain whether the library got out of the planning stage under Demetrius of Phalerum and Ptolemy I. The pair laid the foundation – again, probably literally – but never saw the project develop. Ptolemy I because he died in 283 BC at the ripe old age of eighty-three, and Demetrius because he backed the wrong horse in the succession stakes and was exiled along with his chosen candidate, Ptolemy Keraunos. (While Keraunos was exiled abroad, Demetrius was exiled to the interior where he allegedly perished from snakebite.)

Like many of Ptolemy I's projects, the library gained momentum under Ptolemy II. Texts were purchased from far and wide, and where they could not be purchased they were expropriated. Ships arriving in Alexandria had any books confiscated by customs officials. These texts were given to the library, and copies were promptly made. If the text was considered valuable enough, it was confiscated and the original owner was given the copy and compensation, otherwise the Library returned the book and kept a copy.

Ptolemy was interested in more than the Greek world, and it is known that the Library had a substantial Egyptian section which may well have contained temple records going back thousands of years. There was as large a Mesopotamian section as could be squeezed from the Seleucids, and Eastern writings obtained after Ptolemy II opened diplomatic relations with Ashoka, the Mauryan emperor of India. Ashoka was a proselytizing Buddhist, so there is little doubt that the Library had a fine collection of Buddhist texts.

The poet and scholar Callimachus was given the job of classifying the Library's collection, which is estimated as having eventually grown to almost three-quarters of a million texts. Books were classified by type

– e.g. History, law, medicine, mathematics and tragedies. An index gave title, author, place of origin and the number of lines in the text. Small wonder that by the time of the Romans the writer Vitruvius could refer to the Library as 'The memory of mankind'.

The loss of that Library – partly due to carelessness on the part of Julius Caesar and partly due to Christian fanaticism ('it's not worth keeping if it is not in the Bible, and if it's in the Bible there's no point in keeping it elsewhere', as one bishop noted) – has been mourned by scholars ever since. A later attempt to blame the burning of the scrolls on the Muslims after their conquest of Egypt is particularly perverse, given that it is mostly thanks to preservation in places like Baghdad that many ancient texts survived at all.

One major work of the library has survived intact to the present day. That is the translation of the Old Testament of the Bible from Hebrew to Greek. The text is called the Septuagint in recognition of the seventy scholars who worked on the task. The measure was sponsored by Ptolemy II. Greek was the major language of Alexandria, and it turned out that many second-generation Jews were mostly or entirely Greek-speaking. The translation was necessary if many Jews were to understand their own sacred texts.

There had been considerable debate since as to whether this was an attempt by Ptolemy to preserve the Jewish tradition in Alexandria, or a Hellenizing measure that made it unnecessary for Jews to learn their mother tongue. It is entirely possible also that Ptolemy simply did not think of the matter in those terms, but simply as a benefaction that would make a substantial proportion of his main city happy with his rule.

The Lighthouse at Pharos

To call the Great Lighthouse the most wonderful creation of Ptolemaic Egypt is to be literally correct, as the lighthouse became known as another of the seven wonders of the ancient world. It was literally a beacon of Hellenism, visible for well over a hundred miles out to sea, at night thanks to the fire which burned at the top, and by day thanks to the column of smoke that rose from that same fire.

The lighthouse was built at the mouth of the harbour on the islet of Pharos. Like many of Ptolemy's creations this also was intended as an epic work from the start. The foundation was blocks of stone weighing up to 75 tons apiece, held together with bronze clamps and sealed by molten lead which stopped the waves from forcing the blocks apart. (The remains of the Lighthouse have long since been located underwater, and curious tourists with an aqualung can inspect them in person.)

The tower built atop this massive foundation was at least 120 metres or around 400 feet tall. That's the height of a thirty-storey building. We know from representations on coins that the structure came in two parts. The first was a high rectangular tower with slightly sloping sides. This was already high enough to afford a spectacular view of Alexandria and its environs, and was regularly visited by tourists. The second part was a stretched-out cone rather along the lines of the classic modern lighthouse. We have to assume that this came with some form of winch arrangement for the substantial amounts of wood which the fire consumed every day.

The lighthouse at Pharos was a signal to the Mediterranean world that the port of Alexandria was open for business. Tyre and the Phoenician cities had suffered from the Alexandrian conquest, and Ptolemy was eager for his new city to largely replace the Levantine cities as the major port handling trade from the East. It was also a more secure port. The Levant was also claimed by the Seleucids, while Alexandria was very much a Ptolemaic possession. As a propaganda device demonstrating the power and resources which the Ptolemies were prepared to invest for the public good, the Lighthouse was every bit as much a success as it was effective in its stated purpose of assisting navigation. Even today, in many languages the word for 'lighthouse' is a variant of 'Pharos'.

The lighthouse was typical of Ptolemy I. It was awe-inspiring, yet practical and built on an unprecedented scale. Also like Ptolemy's other projects such as the Library and the canal from the Red Sea, it was too massive a work to be constructed in his own lifetime. Ptolemy built with posterity in mind – not just his monuments, but the entire kingdom. We see the same care taken with improvements to the legal system and agriculture – measures which were not as flashy as his great memorials, but which also served to build a kingdom that was intended to endure.

In fact the lighthouse outlasted the Ptolemies by some distance. It survived intact through the Roman era – and in fact tourist tat from Alexandria depicting the lighthouse are among our best sources for its appearance. Eventually the lighthouse suffered the same fate as its fellow Wonder, the Colossus of Rhodes. About a thousand years ago an earthquake brought down at least the top section of the lighthouse, but the damaged lower portion survived for another three hundred years until another series of quakes destroyed that also.

The Tomb of Alexander

Another powerful propaganda device which helped Ptolemy to position his kingdom at the centre of the Hellenic world was his possession of the body of Alexander. Having Alexander in the kingdom certainly signified that Egypt was among the foremost of Alexander's conquests, but it also gave Ptolemy great status with his peers. In Macedonian tradition a king was formally buried by his successor.

In taking possession of the body of Alexander and afterwards interring the body with a royal funeral, Ptolemy was implicitly stating that he had a claim to Alexander's entire empire. Not that Ptolemy wanted all of Alexander's domains and all the grief that went with ruling them, but given that he could claim the entire empire, no-one was going to dispute the legitimacy of his possession of Egypt.

Alexander was originally buried near Memphis, according to his stated wish that he be buried with his 'father' Zeus in the aspect of Ra-Amun. In 280 BC Ptolemy II decided that the body was too distant to make a proper impact on the Hellenistic world, and asked the appropriate priests whether Alexander would not be happier lying at rest in the city which he had founded. Undoubtedly this question came with the clear inference that the only acceptable answer was 'yes', and indeed the priests did agree that this should be so.

Re-interred in a suitably monumental tomb, the body of Alexander became something between a tourist attraction and a site of pilgrimage. Julius Caesar and Augustus Caesar certainly visited, and it is probable that the burial place became a 'heroon'. These shrines were built over or at least close to the supposed burial places of mythological heroes, and great men of later eras. As such, heroons were already a long-established tradition in the Greek world before the cult of Alexander ever got going. Indeed there was already a heroon established in Macedonia for Alexander's father, Philip II.

What became of Alexander's body is one of the enduring mysteries of the ancient world. Some deny that it ever came to Egypt at all, and twenty-first century archaeologists have found at least two sites that may, at the very least, have been prepared in the expectation that Alexander would be buried there.

If – as is most probable – Alexander was indeed buried in Egypt, then exactly where is unknown. Sources suggest that the site was largely unknown even by late Roman times. In recent years there have been some determined attempts to discover Alexander's whereabouts, but it is highly probable that the heroon became a chapel which became a mosque. No-one is going to dig up a religious building even in the search for a lost hero, so it is quite likely that Alexander will lie quietly in the walled-off basement of an obscure mosque for generations to come.

A lost Ptolemaic city rediscovered

Earlier mention has been made of the Graeco-Egyptian city of Herakleion, named after Hercules, the demi-god whom the two cultures shared in common. For centuries the site of this lost city was unknown.

The first clues as to where the city might be were discovered in the early 1930s. A pilot flying over the Nile delta observed what he thought might be ruins stretching down to the sea. The ruins which survived on land were nothing special in a country which has an abundance of such, but the local authorities sent divers to check what lay beneath the Mediterranean waves. The divers reported that there was nothing there.

After that came the Second World War, and a Middle East where tensions were exacerbated by Cold War rivalries. No-one paid much attention to an obscure pre-war report about an apparent archaeological dead-end until echo-sounding and geology turned up some further details. The most important of these was that the sea bed, once one got through the sand and silt washed down by the Nile, was formed from clay.

This is important because clay has an almost sponge-like ability to absorb water. Like a sponge, when clay is compressed the water is squeezed out. Herakleion had existed peaceably for centuries as a small Egyptian town. With the arrival of the Ptolemies and the opening of new trade routes with the East and the rest of the Mediterranean world, Herakleion became something of a boom town. There was a large increase in population, accompanied by development of the docks, of the temples and the administrative buildings. Literally hundreds of tons were added to the weight pressing down on Herakleion's clay.

The city literally collapsed under the strain. This was no dramatic Atlantis-style deluge, but a slow settling that took place over centuries. By the end of the Ptolemaic era the city was in decline and by around AD 800 flooding had made the site uninhabitable. The rising waters which accompanied the Medieval Warm Period of AD 800–1400 finished the job. By the modern era, all but the far outskirts of Herakleion were underwater.

This slow submersion was accompanied by the slow accretion of layer after layer of mud and sand as the flood waters of the Nile washed over the site. By the time Egyptian divers investigated in the 1930s Herakleion was not only underwater, but buried.

Sadly, the native houses of mud bricks have long dissolved into the waters from which they came, but the monumental statuary of Herakleion has proven a gift that keeps on giving. Among the more massive edifices discovered so far are a 5-metre, 5,500kg statue of the River God Hapi and a massive head of the god Serapis. The remains of dozens of ships have still to be investigated.

In fact, because conditions at the dive site mean that archaeologists can only work for a few months every year, less than ten per cent of the city has so far been investigated. Discoveries such as a black marble stele inscribed with details of the tax system are already changing perceptions of life in Ptolemaic Egypt. Doubtless there is more to come.

Epilogue

The story of the Hellenistic era so far has taken us from the growth of the kingdom of Macedon (an area of a few thousand square kilometres) to a bloc of kingdoms with an area of some five and a half million square kilometres. The Greeks in Asia started out as the inhabitants of largely autonomous coastal cities, and ended up spread thinly across the entire massive region, in cities dotted across the landscape from the highlands of Afghanistan to the upper cataracts of the Nile.

Yet the entire period described in this book, from the birth of Philip II of Macedon in 382 BC to the death of Ptolemy II of Egypt in 246 BC is covered by just two lifetimes of the traditional threescore years and ten. This represents a time of change and disruption virtually unequalled until the modern era. Necessarily, given the amount of history which has been packed between these covers, our focus has been on the essential political and military developments which led to the rise and establishment of the Hellenistic kingdoms.

Yet these developments did not happen in isolation. The conquest of the Achaemenid Persian Empire literally opened up a new world to the Greeks. This could not help but have a massive impact on everything from scientific understanding of the universe to dining habits around the supper table. After Alexander the world was literally never the same again.

A brief summary of the major developments in the early Hellenistic era covers a number of fields.

Philosophy

This we need to divide into two types. The first is the formalized, stratified thinking of men such as Plato and Pythagoras. Even though these men predated the Hellenistic era, their work was extended and modified in this period. However, there was a more general 'philosophy' – the mindset of the average citizen of the Hellenistic kingdoms as the population struggled to cope with a flood of new facts, religions and ideas that changed perceptions of the world.

Faced with such a stimulus a people can either expand their horizons to embrace the new, or retreat, clinging firmly to what they already know. By and large and to their credit, the Hellenistic Greeks took the former course. Alexander the Great set the tone by appearing to explicitly aim for a fusion of Persian and Greek culture. His successors went nowhere near as far, but they by no means rejected the culture of the lands they ruled. Where they stuck to Greek culture and practice, this was not through a belief that the Greeks were a superior people (though they certainly felt that theirs was a superior culture), but because that was what they knew, and they knew it worked.

Where it was better to 'go native' the Hellenistic kings did so with enthusiasm. It is actually remarkable how historians who have insisted that the Hellenistic kings were hell-bent on Greekifying their subjects managed to overlook the many representations of the Ptolemies in full Egyptian dress, or the many benefactions of the Seleucid kings to the temples of Babylonian and other non-Greek gods.

A good metaphor for the overall adaptation of the Greeks to their new world was Koine – that somewhat simplified version of Greek which became the *lingua franca* of the East (and therefore the language of the first Gospels). No-one was compelled to learn the language, and there were no punishments for not speaking it. Yet once past a certain social level one needed Koine, not just for the transaction of official business (the Rosetta Stone remains today as testimony to how far the Hellenistic kings went to make sure that they accommodated the many different languages of their kingdoms) but also for private business with non-Greeks elsewhere in the empire.

Likewise with religion. Generally locals and Greeks sought aspects where their gods could be identified as the same entities. Hercules was far from the only deity to have worshippers in very different cultures. Zeus and Ra-Amun were conflated, and in Asia Minor the syncretism of Artemis with dozens of local deities led to the goddess becoming the patron deity of much of Anatolia. Where no pair of gods from different pantheons could be shoehorned together, a new deity was promoted to do the job, Serapis from Egypt being the outstanding example.

Among the formal disciplines of philosophy, Cynicism and Stoicism gained followers because they moved away from wider views of the nature of the universe and the development of mankind and turned inward to the self. Perhaps the most famous of the Cynics was Diogenes of Sinope, who took the idea of rejecting worldly possessions and desires to their logical extreme by living half-naked in a barrel. (Who possessed the barrel is unknown.) Alexander the Great came to pay his respects, and knew his man too well to expect Diogenes to rise from where he was sprawled out in the sunshine.

'I am here to bestow upon you whatever you desire', Alexander allegedly informed Diogenes. Diogenes contemplated the man who could give provinces, palaces, concubines and gold by the waggon load. 'Do this for me then', said Diogenes, 'move aside. You are blocking my sunlight.' Alexander later remarked, 'were I not Alexander, I should wish to be Diogenes'.

The Stoics had the same approach to life, but approached it more carefully. For them it was acceptable for a Stoic to own possessions (which was just as well, for in later years the stoic Marcus Aurelius AD 121–180 had the whole Roman Empire) but the possessions should not own the Stoic. Stoics believed that so long as a person had conquered his or her inner demons, the rest of the world did not matter.

Stoicism was founded by one Zeno of Citium (340–260 BC). A wealthy merchant, possibly of Phoenician stock, Zeno was attracted to the teachings of Socrates. He began teaching on the porch (stoa) of one of the colonnades in the Athenian agora, and it is from this stoa that the philosophy derives its name. Antigonus II Gonatas was an admirer who always visited Zeno when he was in Athens and tried unsuccessfully to persuade the philosopher to move to Macedon.

Zeno was succeeded by the philosopher Cleanthes who demonstrated his stoic credentials by keeping his other job as a water-carrier until he became head of the Stoic school. Cleanthes made important intellectual advances in both physics and ethics, but his main achievement was in training his successor Chrysippus, who developed Zeno's ideas to the degree that has him called 'the second founder of stoicism'.

A competing philosophy which long outlasted the Hellenistic kingdoms also originated in our period. This was Epicureanism, named after its founder Epicurus (341–270 BC). Epicurus was bounced about by the wars of the Diadochi, having done military service in Athens and then joining his parents in Asia Minor after they were forcibly transplanted by Perdiccas. He taught in Lampascus, a city on the Hellespont, before returning to Athens in around 306 BC. Epicurus had a typically Hellenistic view of the world. He believed that the fate of gods and men was ruled by chance, and that the gods neither punished nor rewarded humans. Death was the end for body and spirit, so in life humans should strive only to enjoy its pleasures and be free from anxiety.

Warfare

Hellenistic warfare remained based on the combination of pike phalanx and cavalry pioneered by Philip II and perfected by Alexander. However, while the equipment remained the same, there were some changes in the men who rode the horses and wielded the pikes. Phalangites were a commodity in desperately short supply in all the Hellenistic kingdoms, and there was fierce competition to recruit them. It became usual practice for a victorious king to immediately recruit any enemy phalangites who fell into his hands after a successful battle. This led to a degree of civility in inter-Hellenistic warfare, as the participants in a conflict not only shared the language and religion of their opponents, but might later that same war be sharing their dinner and a tent.

Hellenistic armies were vastly larger than their Classical counterparts. While 6,000 men was a very respectable army in the period before the Persian wars, a post-Alexander army needed at least 20,000 men to be taken seriously. Armies of over 80,000 were not uncommon. This meant that the armies of the Hellenistic kings were generally supplemented by whatever specialist troops the region had to offer. As noted earlier (p.137) the Seleucid kingdom was particularly rich in a diverse range of cavalry types, and Syria also produced bowmen to rival the skilled archers of Crete. All sides had a corps of elephants. These the Seleucids sourced from India, while Ptolemy used the smaller (now extinct) North African elephant. The Macedonians scrounged theirs from wherever they could.

With many aspects of the Hellenistic world, the kings borrowed from the Classical era and supersized it. This was also true of warfare. Demetrios Poliorcetes, son of Antigonus Monophthalmus was famous for the size of his siege engines, his masterpiece being the monster produced for the unsuccessful siege of Rhodes, which stood ten stories tall and bristled with catapults and dart-throwers.

Naval warfare was important during this entire period, as control of the Aegean significantly affected the military reach of the Hellenistic powers. Not only were warships produced in epic numbers, but there was a degree of one-upmanship among the Hellenistic kings as each strove to produce ships that were bigger, longer and more powerful than those of their rivals. The basic trireme of the Persian wars was generally replaced by the quinquereme, though it is highly unlikely that this involved five banks of oars since later productions went all the way up to the decereme.

Whatever these were, the trend towards bigger warships was already established under Alexander the Great who ordered septiremes to be prepared for naval operations around Arabia (which were cancelled on his death). In part this trend towards larger warships was because of the same development that had allowed active siege operations on land. The development of catapults and dart throwers had changed the warship from the sleek and manoeuvrable ramming device of the Peloponnesian War to a bulky floating missile platform.

Where once ships circled, looking for a chance to ram one another, now they bombarded their opponents with missiles, seeking to penetrate their opponent's hull, but also to massacre the sailors and marines close-packed on the decks waiting to swarm aboard a disabled enemy ship.

Art and literature

Hellenistic art was long decried as a step down from the unequalled glory of the Classical era. Yet here too, a reappraisal is needed. Classical sculpture focussed on the ideal, with perfectly proportioned bodies staring serenely into the infinite. Hellenistic art was closer to that of the Roman Republic in that it aimed at realism, with very human – sometimes even grotesque – individuals in the grip of strong emotion.

The sculpture of The Dying Gaul (carved to celebrate the victory of Attalus of Pergamum over the Galatians) or the Nike of Samothrace depicting the winged goddess of victory about to take flight are eloquent testimony that Hellenistic sculpture possessed its own power and beauty. Archaeology has also helped to overturn long-entrenched prejudices by demonstrating that the jewellery and architecture of the Hellenistic era remained of an exquisite standard, despite the Hellenistic tendency to build big.

Three of the seven wonders of the ancient world belong to the Hellenistic era: the Colossus of Rhodes (p.72); the lighthouse at Pharos (p.148) and the Temple of Artemis at Ephesus, burned down the day Alexander the Great was born and rebuilt in the decades that followed. (Some of the columns from this temple can be seen today in the Hagia Sophia in Istanbul.) These three structures alone should successfully detonate the idea that the Hellenistic era was a period of stagnation and decline.

If we are to accept the Hellenistic opinion of their own literary abilities, then literature was in decline. Certainly the age produced no Thucydides, Euripides or Aristophanes. Nevertheless, some solid additions were made to the corpus of ancient Greek writing. There are for instance, the bucolic poems of Theocritus, a poet who moved to Alexandria, and Kallimachos who produced a massive corpus of criticism and commentary on Classical authors. Kallimachos was recruited to Alexandria under Ptolemy II and became one of the foremost scholars at the library. Apollonius of Rhodes seems to have worked with Kallimachos at the Library. His epic poem, the *Argonautica* has survived, and supplies much of what is known today about the legend of Jason and the Golden Fleece.

If most early Hellenistic literature was centred on the Library at Alexandria, an exception was comedy. This, like philosophy, remained with its centre in Athens. The leading exponent of Hellenistic-era comedy was Menander, a mannered aristocrat who wrote a good number of plays, only one of which has survived intact.

Menander's main rival was one Philemon, whose works have not survived at all other than as fragments and a list of titles. Philemon was briefly lured to Alexandria by Ptolemy II but returned to work in Athens. Philemon's life spanned most of the early Hellenistic era. He was born in 362 BC when the Persian Empire was still going strong under king Artaxerxes II, and he died just short of his hundredth birthday in 262 BC, the year that Antiochus II took over the Seleucid Empire.

Philemon probably came from Cilicia in Asia Minor. Theocritus was from Sicily, and Kallimachos was from Cyrene in North Africa. Apollonius was from the island of Rhodes, and all may have met at the library of Alexandria in Egypt. This international constellation of talent was often reproduced on a smaller scale across the Hellenistic world – a world where ideas, no less than people, moved freely between the kingdoms, no matter what rivalries might have existed between the rulers themselves.

Select Bibliography

Bagnall, R (Ed), *Hellenistic Egypt: Monarchy, Society, Economy, Culture* (University of California Press, 2007).

Bar-Kochva, B, *The Seleucid Army: Organization and Tactics in the Great Campaigns* (Cambridge University Press, 1979).

Bevan, E, *The House of Ptolemy: A History of Hellenistic Egypt Under the Ptolemaic Dynasty* (Ares Publishers, 1985).

Cartledge, P, *Alexander the Great* (Vintage, 2005)

Cawkwell, G, 'Review of Marsden 1964 "The Campaign of Gaugamela", *The Classical Review*, Vol. 15, No. 2 (1965).

Chaniotis, A, *War in the Hellenistic world: A social and cultural history* (Malden, MA, and Blackwell, 2005).

Coskun, A, 'Deconstructing a Myth Of Seleucid History: The So-Called "Elephant Victory" Revisited', *Phoenix* 66, pp. 57–73 (2012).

Doty, T, *Cuneiform Archives from Hellenistic Uruk* (Ann Arbor (diss.), 1977).

Engels, D, *Alexander the Great and the Logistics of the Macedonian Army* (University of California Press, 2012).

Grainger, J, *Seleukos Nikator* (Routledge, 1990).

Grainger, J, *The Rise of the Seleukid Empire* (Pen & Sword).

Grainger, J, *Kings and Kingship in the Hellenistic World 350–30 BC* (Pen and Sword, 2017).

Green, P, *Alexander to Actium: The Evolution of the Hellenistic Age* (University of California Press, 1990).

Hadley, R, 'Royal Propaganda of Seleucus I and Lysimachus', *JHS* 94 (1974), pp. 50–65.

Hammond, N. 'The battle of the Granicus River', *Journal of Hellenic Studies*, vol 100, pp. 73–88, 1980.

Heinen, H, 'The Syrian Egyptian Wars and the New Kingdoms of Asia Minor', in *CAH2*, VII pt.1, pp. 412–445.

Holt, F, *Thundering Zeus: The Making of Hellenistic Bactria* (Berkeley, 1999).

Kuhrt, A, & S Sherwin-White (eds), *Hellenism in the East* (Duckworth, 1987).

Lampros, S, *Greece-The Hellenistic Age* (Milliken, 1969).

Lewis, N, *The Greeks in Ptolemaic Egypt (Classics in Papyrology)* (American Society of Papyrologists, 2001).

Macurdy, G, *Hellenistic Queens* (Ares Publishers reprint, 1932).

Momigliano, A, *Alien Wisdom: The Limits of Hellenization* (Cambridge University Press, 1975).

Narain, A, *The Indo-Greeks* (Oxford University Press, 1957).

Sherwin-White, S, and A Kurht, *From Samarkhand to Sardis: A New Approach to the Seleucid Empire* (California University Press, 1993).

Shipley, G, *The Greek World after Alexander: 323–30 BC* (Routledge, 2000).

Worthington, I, *Ptolemy I: King and Pharaoh of Egypt* (Oxford University Press, 2016).

Index